Sentimental Education
The Complexity of Disenchantment

TWAYNE'S MASTERWORK STUDIES
ROBERT LECKER, GENERAL EDITOR

Sentimental Education
The Complexity of Disenchantment

William Paulson

Twayne Publishers • New York
Maxwell Macmillan Canada • Toronto
Maxwell Macmillan International • New York Oxford Singapore Sydney

Twayne's Masterwork Studies No. 85

Sentimental Education: The Complexity of Disenchantment
William Paulson

Twayne Publishers   Maxwell Macmillan Canada, Inc.
Macmillan Publishing Company   1200 Eglinton Avenue East
866 Third Avenue   Suite 200
New York, New York 10022   Don Mills, Ontario M3C 3N1

Macmillan Publishing Company is part of the Maxwell Communication Group
of Companies.

Library of Congress Cataloging-in-Publication Data

Paulson, William R., 1955-
    Sentimental education : the complexity of disenchantment / William
Paulson.
        p. cm. — (Twayne's masterwork studies ; no. 85)
    Includes bibliographical references and index.
    ISBN 0-8057-9428-X (alk. paper) — ISBN 0-8057-8568-X
(pbk. : alk. paper)
    1. Flaubert, Gustave, 1821-1880. Education sentimentale.
I. Title. II. Series.
PQ2246.E5P38   1992
843'.8—dc20   91-34023
                                                            CIP

10 9 8 7 6 5 4 3 2 1 (nc)
10 9 8 7 6 5 4 3 2 1 (pb)

Printed in the United States of America

For Lionel Gossman

Contents

Note on the References
and Acknowledgments

All references to *Sentimental Education* in this book are to the English translation by Robert Baldick (Penguin Books, 1964). Translations of material cited from French editions are my own.

I gratefully acknowledge grants from the College of Literature, Science, and the Arts and the Office of the Vice-President for Research at the University of Michigan.

It is a pleasure to thank the people who have helped me with this book. My largest debt of gratitude is owed to my research assistant, Marguerite Walter, who not only worked in the library and surveyed secondary literature, but also contributed greatly to my thinking and writing through her many insightful comments and suggestions. I also wish to thank Jacques Neefs, who took the time to introduce me to the Flaubert collection at the Institut des Textes et Manuscrits Modernes in Paris, and Elizabeth MacArthur, whose help in securing the frontispiece illustration was invaluable. The students with whom I have read *Sentimental Education,* both at Mount Holyoke College and at the University of Michigan, shaped my approach to the novel and were often in my thoughts as I wrote.

Gustave Flaubert as a young man, by Delaunay.
Photograph courtesy of the Bibliothèque Nationale, Paris

Chronology:
Gustave Flaubert's Life and Works

1821   Gustave Flaubert is born 12 December in Rouen, where his father is the chief surgeon at the main hospital.

1830   The restored Bourbon monarchy is overthrown in a Paris revolution 27–29 July. Louis-Philippe d'Orléans becomes "King of the French" in a new, constitutional regime often called the July Monarchy.

1831   In January Flaubert begins mentioning his writings—principally plays—in letters to his friend Ernest Chevalier. With the exception of a few school compositions, the earliest of Flaubert's writings to survive date from 1835.

1836   During the summer, meets and falls in love with Elisa Schlésinger, 26, whose husband, Maurice, is a music publisher. Flaubert never renounces his quasi-platonic attachment for her; he frequents the Schlésinger couple during his student years in Paris and occasionally exchanges letters and visits with Elisa until at least 1872.

1839   Writes to Ernest Chevalier: "But don't think that I'm undecided on the choice of a station in life. I am firmly resolved to have none . . . . Yet if ever I take an active part in the world it will be as a thinker and demoralizer. I will merely tell the truth, but it will be horrible, cruel, and naked."

1840   Receives his Baccalauréat (secondary school diploma) in August.

1841   With no enthusiasm for the subject or the career it could lead to, Flaubert begins his lackluster studies of law in November.

1842   Moves to Paris in July. In October, completes *Novembre* (*November*), a semiautobiographical novel, at once sensual and despairing.

1843   Begins writing a novel called *L'Education sentimentale* (*Sentimental Education*) in February, which begins as a story of the social and amorous initiation of a young provincial, Henry, who comes to Paris to study law.

1844   Suffers an epileptic attack in January and abandons his legal studies, returning to live with his family and devote himself to the life of writing that he seems to have always wanted. In June, the family moves to a house at Croisset, outside Rouen, which will be Flaubert's home until his death.

1845   Completes the first *Sentimental Education* in January. The emphasis has shifted, in the latter chapters, from the worldly and superficial Henry to his friend Jules, who becomes a serious literary artist, devoted to impersonal representation and ideal beauty.

1846   In January, Flaubert's father dies. In March, Flaubert's beloved sister Caroline dies from childbirth fever. Henceforth, he will live with his mother and his niece, named Caroline after her mother. In July, begins his often stormy liaison with Louise Colet, to whom he will write many of his most famous and eloquent letters, especially during the writing of *Madame Bovary*. Writes to Louise Colet: "Someday I will write all that, the modern young man, whose soul blossoms at sixteen through an immense love that makes him lust for luxury, glory, all the splendors of life, this sad and streaming poetry of the adolescent's heart—there is a new string that no one has set vibrating."

1848   A revolution in Paris 22–24 February topples Louis-Philippe's July Monarchy and establishes the Second Republic. Flaubert writes to Louise Colet in March: "You ask my opinion about what has just happened. Well then! it's all very funny.... I'm profoundly delighted by observing all the crushed ambitions. I don't know whether the new form of government and the resulting social order will be favorable to Art." National elections send to Paris a conservative National Assembly in April, hostile to the Parisian working class and to many of the original aims of the February revolution. The government uses the army to crush a workers' insurrection in Paris 23–26 June, killing thousands. Louis-Napoleon Bonaparte, nephew of Napoleon I, elected President of the French Republic by universal suffrage in December.

1849   Completes *La Tentation de saint Antoine* (*The Temptation of Saint Anthony*), but, on the advice of his friends Louis Bouilhet and Maxime Du Camp, refrains from trying to publish it. Leaves

Chronology: Gustave Flaubert's Life and Works

	Paris in October with Du Camp for a two-year voyage to the Orient, beginning with Egypt.
1851	Returns to France in June after stays in Greece and Italy on the return journey from the Near East. Begins writing *Madame Bovary* in September. Bonaparte dissolves the National Assembly 2 December and assumes full power in a coup d'état; a year later, following a plebiscite, he will be proclaimed Emperor Napoleon III, inaugurating the Second Empire.
1853	Writes to Louise Colet of his youth: "Between the world and me there was a kind of stained glass window, yellow with fiery stripes and gold arabesques, so that everything reflected on my soul, as on the stone floor of a decorated sanctuary, transfigured and yet melancholic . . . . When I am old, I will warm myself by writing all that. I will be like those who, before leaving on a long voyage, say farewell to graves they hold dear; before I die I will revisit my dreams."
1854	In May, ends his relationship with Louise Colet.
1856	In April, finishes writing *Madame Bovary*, which is published in installments in a review from October to December, and in book form in April 1857. Works on a second version of *La Tentation de saint Antoine*, but publishes only fragments of it.
1857	During January and February, Flaubert tried and acquitted on charges of "offenses to public morality and religion" for the publication of *Madame Bovary*. In March, writes about himself to Mademoiselle Leroyer de Chantepie, an unsung novelist and fan of *Madame Bovary*: "I too have voluntarily refused myself love, happiness—Why? I don't know. It was perhaps out of pride—or out of fright?" In September, begins writing *Salammbô*, a historical novel set in ancient Carthage.
1858	Travels to North Africa (present-day Algeria and Tunisia) from April to June to research the setting of *Salammbô*.
1862	Completes and publishes *Salammbô*. Sometime between March and July, begins a scenario for a novel called *Madame Moreau*, which will become *L'Education sentimentale*. Until 1864, he will hesitate between this project and the work that will come to be *Bouvard et Pécuchet* (*Bouvard and Pécuchet*).
1863	Begins writing to George Sand, who will be his most important correspondent until her death in 1876.
1864	In September, begins writing "a novel of modern life, set in Paris"—*L'Education sentimentale*. During October, describes the work he has started to Mademoiselle Leroyer de Chantepie:

"I want to write the moral history—*sentimental* would be truer—of the men of my generation. It's a book of love, of passion, but of passion as it can now exist, that is to say, inactive. The subject, as I've conceived it, is, I believe, profoundly true, but because of just that, probably not very entertaining. Facts and drama are somewhat lacking, and the action is spread over too long a time period."

1867   Writes to George Sand: "As for the book I'm writing, I fear that its conception is faulty, and nothing can be done about that; will such listless characters interest anyone? Great effects are only realized with simple things, clear-cut passions. But I see nothing simple anywhere in the modern world."

1869   Writes in April to George Sand: "Here is the title I've adopted for my novel, in desperation: *L'Education sentimentale, Histoire d'un jeune homme* (*Story of a Young Man*). I'm not saying that it's good, but so far it's the one that best expresses the book's thought." Completes the manuscript of his novel 16 May, 4:56 a.m. Shaken by the death of Louis Bouilhet, his closest friend and literary adviser, in July Flaubert writes to Jules Duplan: "I say to myself, 'What's the use of writing anymore, since he's no longer there?'" *L'Education sentimentale* is published in November to mixed, often unfavorable, reviews.

1870   The Franco-Prussian War, fought between July and September, brings the downfall of the Second Empire. In December, Prussian troops are billeted in Flaubert's home, and he is severely demoralized by his country's defeat and the hardships of the occupation.

1872   Flaubert's mother dies in April. In October, he writes to Madame Schlésinger: "*Ma vieille Amie, ma vieille Tendresse,* . . . For me the future has no more dreams, but the days of yesteryear appear as though bathed in a golden mist. Against that luminous background where beloved phantoms reach out to me, the face that stands out most splendidly is—yours.—Yes, yours . . . . Let us write to each other from time to time, if only a word, so as to know that we are still alive." Begins writing *Bouvard et Pécuchet* in August, a ferocious (yet also comic) satire of stupidity and human knowledge.

1874   Publishes a third, much-shortened version of *La Tentation de saint Antoine*. His play about politics, *Le Candidat* (*The Candidate*), closes after only four performances.

1875   Sets aside *Bouvard et Pécuchet* to begin work on *Trois contes* (*Three Tales*): *Un coeur simple* (*A Simple Heart*), *La Légende de*

Saint Julien l'Hospitalier (*Saint Julian the Hospitaler*), and *Hérodias*. Sacrificing his fortune to save his niece and her husband from ruin, Flaubert loses his financial security and must worry about money for the rest of his life.

1876   George Sand dies in June. Flaubert later writes to her son: "I began *Un coeur simple* solely for her, only to please her. She died when I was in the middle of my work. Thus it is with all our dreams."

1877   Publishes *Trois contes* in April. Resumes work on *Bouvard et Pécuchet* in June.

1879   Deeply humiliated, but realizing that he has no choice, Flaubert accepts a modest state pension obtained through the influence of his literary friends.

1880   Dies 8 May at his Croisset home. *Bouvard et Pécuchet,* nearly completed, is published the following year.

Literary and Historical Context

1

Historical Context

Sentimental Education is Flaubert's attempt to use fiction to write the moral and sentimental history of his generation, a history steeped in early disenchantment and broken by the revolution of 1848 and its dismal aftermath. The generation born around 1820 reached maturity during the lackluster years of Louis-Philippe's bourgeois monarchy, and many of its members felt a sense of belatedness at having been too young to participate directly in the "three glorious days" of the July 1830 revolution and in the cultural battles of the romantic movement around the same time. Nonetheless, the 1840s were a decade of increasing social ferment, and the uprising that deposed Louis-Philippe in February 1848 seemed at first to be both a fulfillment of reformist hopes and a gateway to utopian dreams. The events that followed, however, quickly brought painful disillusion: the election of a conservative National Assembly in April dashed the hope that universal suffrage would be a progressive political force, and the violent crushing of a workers' uprising in June shattered the dream that political reform led by the bourgeoisie and supported by the working class could lead to a more egalitarian and harmonious society. The coup d'état of 2 December 1851, by which President Louis-Napoleon Bonaparte seized power from the National Assembly, was merely the culmination of a turn to authoritarian rule, and the Republic's supporters were too weary or divided to offer effective resistance.

The Second Empire, which effectively began with the coup d'état but which was officially proclaimed a year later, was a period of economic growth and political quiescence. Until 1860, the repression of the labor movement and of opposition political activity was very severe; virtually no political debate occurred and censorship was strict. In 1857, the century's two most influential works of literary modernism were published and put on trial for outrage to public morals: Flaubert's *Madame Bovary* and Charles Baudelaire's collection of poems, *Les Fleurs du mal* (*Flowers of Evil*). Helped by his family's respectability and by an eloquent, influential defense lawyer, Flaubert won acquittal, but Baudelaire was convicted of obscenity and six of his poems were ordered expunged from subsequent editions of his collection, a judgment not officially reversed until 1949.

Both authors had been severely disillusioned by the events of 1848–51, and their estrangement from the political and social order surely contributed to the qualities that the authorities found so disturbing in their writings. Soon after the coup d'état, Baudelaire wrote that "the 2d of December has physically depoliticized me," and in September 1853, Flaubert gave this bleak assessment of where the shocks of history had left French society: "89 [i.e., the French Revolution] demolished the royalty and the nobility, 48 the bourgeoisie and 51 *the people*. There is *nothing* more but a vulgar and stupid rabble. We are all sunken to the same level of general mediocrity."[1] In effect, Flaubert was saying, no social class has any political or cultural legitimacy. No individual or group can be proposed as a model for society or as a source of positive change because all are simply pursuing their own interests, which are selfish and culturally undistinguished. What probably most upset the authorities about *Madame Bovary* is Flaubert's implicit representation of this absence of cultural legitimacy and moral example. Emma Bovary is a deluded consumer of romantic fiction and an adulteress, but no character in the novel is more lucid or better than she. None has the right to condemn her, and the narrator abstains from doing so. Countless novels had

4

portrayed characters more foolish or depraved than Emma, and many authors had been far less chaste than Flaubert in their eroticism, but *Madame Bovary* scandalized the state and the conservative bourgeoisie by presenting a fictional world with no moral fixed points, no examples of virtue, and no major characters who rise above self-delusion or petty self-interest.

Shortly after finishing *Sentimental Education,* Flaubert wrote to George Sand that, "Since 1815, almost nothing has been done [in politics] except to fight over the exterior form that should be given to the fantastic and odious being called the State."[2] His words reflect not only his own disgust with politics, but also the profound and durable crisis of legitimacy that shook France from the Revolution of 1789 until at least the consolidation of the Third Republic around 1880. For much of that period, a substantial minority or even majority of the French were opposed in principle to the kind of regime under which they lived. The Bourbon Restoration (1814–1830, interrupted in 1815 by Napoleon's Hundred-Days return) was not only condemned as reactionary by supporters of a republic, it was also seen by many patriots—especially those who admired the Napoleonic conquests—as a humiliating regime imposed on France by its enemies.

The July Monarchy placated a few bourgeois republicans by adopting the tricolor flag of the French Revolution and Empire and by increasing somewhat the number of wealthy males eligible to vote, but it never succeeded in its task of national reconciliation. To most partisans of a republic, Louis-Philippe had usurped a revolution whose goal had been the overthrow of the monarchy and not merely a change in dynasty from Bourbon to Orléans. Moreover, with the old aristocracy out of power, it became clear that henceforth the major form of political and social inequality was to be economic and that the July Monarchy was going to govern in the interest of the wealthy commercial class. To the urban workers and their sympathizers, the violent suppression of strikes and uprisings in the early 1830s proved that a government dominated by business interests would be hostile to social progress. To patriots and Bonapartists, Louis-Philippe's cautious and pro-English foreign policy was a form of national dishonor; to artists, bohemians, and aristocrats, the king's own middle-class ways were a symbol of mediocrity. All these griefs come together in the first two parts of *Sentimental Education* in the discussions in which the novel's young men vent their frustrations upon the government.

Economically, the Restoration and July Monarchy were periods of stagnation, during which commercial interests gained increasing political power but industrialization and economic development proceeded slowly. Culturally, however, these were rich and exciting periods in France; the romantic movement of the 1820s and 1830s— exuberant, idealistic, and sentimental—was self-consciously a symbolic protest against the social constraint and calculating materialism of the age. Romanticism was primarily the creation of a cultivated and privileged elite, but its preoccupations were not narrowly elitist: national history, popular traditions, and social or political problems were among its major themes and concerns. Alphonse de Lamartine and Victor Hugo wrote major poems on the social mission of the poet, whom they believed was called to lead humanity on the path to a just and harmonious society.

The decade of the 1840s, during which most of *Sentimental Education* is set, was a period of transition, both economic and cultural.[3] The economy grew more rapidly than in previous decades; roads were better and literacy on the increase. Production of coal, iron, and steel, spurred in part by the Railroad Act of 1842, advanced considerably, although France's Industrial Revolution continued to lag behind that of England. In literature and the arts, the synthesis that many romantics had attempted between elite aesthetic sensibility and progressive humanitarianism began to show signs of strain. The use of the serial novel in mass-circulation newspapers, begun in 1836, made literature into a popular entertainment and led to outcries from purists that the cultural value of writing was being sacrificed to the lowest common denominator of taste in the interest of profit. Similar disdain was not infrequently expressed during the 1840s for "social romanticism" (works that treated the condition of common people, often with a political agenda) and for the works of the few workers and peasants who wrote about their condition and aspirations. As early as 1835, an elitist "art-for-art's-sake" reaction against attempts to fuse beauty and social utility found expression in Théophile Gautier's preface to his novel *Mademoiselle de Maupin.* For Gautier, artists had only the mission of creating new beauty and, accordingly, should leave aside the temptation of providing moral, social, and humanitarian lessons.

During the last years of the July Monarchy, artists and writers became increasingly interested in evoking the experiences of modern life and in portraying characters and events that had previously been considered too ordinary or uninspiring to be worthwhile aesthetic subjects. These tendencies, which gave rise to the terms *modernism* and *realism,* became more evident during the Second Empire. Railroads, the changing face of Paris, the difficulties of starving artists, and the lives of domestic servants were among the new literary and artistic topics that would have seemed quite out of place to the romantic writers of the previous generation. No less important than these changes in theme were the formal innovations of the modernist writers: literary writing, which had long been regarded as a widely shared idiom of communication embellished by rhetorical figures and enlivened by slight variations of personal style, began to appear as a creative performance by which each writer asserted a unique relation to language, literature, and society. Flaubert disdained the "realism" of ordinary or vulgar subjects, but his commitment to a distinguished and uniquely artistic style was a cornerstone of his work. The distinctive and intense style of *Madame Bovary,* like that of *Les Fleurs du mal,* probably contributed to the feelings of disquiet and scandal that led to their authors' prosecution.

After *Madame Bovary,* Flaubert, declaring himself more disgusted than ever with modern life in general and with the bourgeoisie in particular, turned to ancient Carthage for the subject of his next novel, *Salammbô.* If he was condemned to live in a petty and antiartistic age, he implied, he would at least escape from it in his work. With *Sentimental Education,* however, he decided to carry out his long-meditated project of writing the novel of the "modern young man," the story of his generation's struggles to fit into an uninspiring and changing world. He may even have hoped to contribute some insight into the country's social and moral condition. In 1871, standing before the ruins of the public buildings destroyed during the Paris Commune, he is reported to have exclaimed, "All this could have been avoided if people had understood *Sentimental Education.*"

2

The Importance of the Work

Flaubert, more than any other writer, established once and for all the artistic seriousness of the novel, and *Sentimental Education* is his most ambitious work. A generation earlier in France, Honoré de Balzac tried to proclaim the novel to be the major literary form of the modern age, but his claim rested primarily on the vastness of his output and the variety of his subject matter. Balzac was a prodigious observer and analyst, but an indifferent stylist, and it remained for Flaubert to prove, with *Madame Bovary,* that a long work of prose fiction could be as distinguished a literary composition as any tragedy or poem. Henry James wrote that Flaubert was the novelist most admired by other novelists because his example had effectively secured literary honor for their collective enterprise.[4]

During the writing of *Madame Bovary,* Flaubert wrote with pride to Louise Colet that his novel would not contain "a *single* flabby sentence" (*Pléiade,* 2:248). More than simply the achievement of good writing, however, was at stake: Flaubert's aesthetic of the novel demanded a continuous and seamless fusion of style and subject matter, ultimately the abolition of the traditional dichotomy between form and content. "Form and idea, for me, are entirely one, and I don't know what each would be without the other," he wrote to Mademoiselle Leroyer de Chantepie in 1857 (*Pléiade*, 2:785). Instead of a narrative voice, which can be used to tell any story, Flaubert sought (and largely achieved) a style constantly shaped to, and shaping, fictional events to which it was inextricably bound. His unfulfilled dream, in fact, was to make style supremely important and even autonomous: "What seems beautiful to me, what I should like to write, is a book about nothing, a book dependent on nothing external, which would be held together by the internal strength of its style, just as the earth, suspended in the void, depends on nothing external for its support; a book which would have almost no subject, or at least in which the subject would be almost invisible, if such a thing is possible."[5] That such a project was conceivable to Flaubert is testimony to the remarkable "internal strength" of his own style; it also defines the aspect of his writing that can be said to prefigure the postmodern sense of the novel as *text*, as an adventure in writing rather than the written telling of a story.

Flaubert's novels, however, have subjects, and the singularity and importance of *Sentimental Education* stems from the fact that its subject is nothing less than the disenchantment of a generation during a decisive and complex period of history. The struggle of an exemplary young man to come to terms with his society is arguably *the* major novelistic subject of the nineteenth century, with representative works including Stendhal's *The Red and the Black*, Balzac's *Lost Illusions*, and Dickens's *Great Expectations*. Nowhere except in *Sentimental Education*, however, is this large subject matched by a style so cannily wrought that it might support a book with almost no subject at all.

Moreover, Flaubert's preoccupation with style, far from distracting him from the historical and social dimensions of his work, was accompanied by an equally strong obsession with fidelity to the world outside the text. Historians and sociologists admire *Sentimental Education* for the exceptional quality of its documentation and the pertinence of its insights into the interactions between social class and ideology. Flaubert's concern with being true to the things he wrote about led him to scour newspapers from 1847 in search of topics of then-current political conversation, to have himself driven through the Fontainebleau forest, and to ask a friend for a detailed account of the public transportation available between Fontainebleau and Paris in June 1848. To do less, he believed, would be to falsify reality and thus to diminish the truth and force of his work. In the youthful novel to which Flaubert gave the name *L'Education sentimentale* 25 years before completing his mature work, the young artist Jules defends this kind of fidelity to reality in a way that remains pertinent to the novel of 1869: "He had come to see that whatever eliminates restricts, whatever selects omits, whatever prunes destroys ... if a writer conceives the past otherwise than it actually was, adjusting the facts and modifying the participants to suit himself, the result will be a false and lifeless work."[6] The novelist's ultimate aim, for Flaubert, is not to copy reality. He believed that a novel gains in internal cohesion by accepting, rather than eliminating or falsifying, the constraints of the real world as its author can best understand them.

In the case of *Sentimental Education,* the result of this method is a kaleidoscopic evocation of a society in disarray. The novel's episodes and images often reflect and reduplicate one another, and yet these patterns are never static correspondences, for they are displaced and transformed by the continuous movement of time's passage. The growing experience and disenchantment of the characters parallel the irreversible transformation of their society, which is shaped by the ebb and flow of reform and conservatism and fissured by the shocks of revolution and reaction.

Meticulous composition, the drama of nineteenth-century history, and a singular position in the development of the novel are not, however, the only reasons why *Sentimental Education* continues to live and find new readers equal to its challenges. The novel's world—the manner in which its form interprets the society of its time—can in many important respects stand as a commentary on today's society, at least in the wealthy developed nations of the West. The careers of Frédéric Moreau and his friends raise questions about how to live in a society dominated by money and bereft of valid ideals, in which reform is driven by narcissistic resentments and dreams, and conservatism embraced out of cynical self-interest. These questions are no less pertinent—and no easier—now than in Flaubert's era, and *Sentimental Education* provides no direct answers to them; perhaps no answers at all. Its achievement lies not in satisfying

11

our desire for simple answers, but in provoking us to understand the world's complexity and the predicaments of those who drift or struggle in it. "The novel's spirit is the spirit of complexity," writes Milan Kundera, the author of *Immortality* and *The Unbearable Lightness of Being*. "Every novel says to the reader: 'Things are not as simple as you think.' That is the novel's eternal truth."[7] It may also be the most timely lesson of *Sentimental Education*.

3

Critical Reception

Sentimental Education has always been a difficult and controversial book. Its entry in a present-day equivalent of Flaubert's *Dictionary of Accepted Ideas* might go something like this: "*Sentimental Education*— unreadable and boring. The greatest French novel of the nineteenth century. Subtler and more complex than *Madame Bovary*. Lacks *Bovary*'s intriguing plot and well-drawn characters." Unlike *Madame Bovary*, which was acknowledged to be a masterpiece when it appeared and has always retained that reputation, Flaubert's "Story of a Young Man" has had detractors no less eloquent and illustrious than its defenders.

Flaubert himself had misgivings about the structure of his novel and about the potential interest of its characters to readers. In August 1866, he complained to a friend that it would take him three more years to finish it and that "it may prove to be a mediocre work, because the conception is faulty. ... My purpose is complex—a bad aesthetic method" (*Letters*, 2:81–2). It must be noted, however, that these reservations disappear from his letters during the last year of the writing. We have no record of how he judged the finished work during the months before its publication on 17 November 1869, but he was clearly annoyed by the negative reviews, despite his conviction that journalistic criticism was unworthy of his attention. "I don't care in the least," he wrote to George Sand on 3 December, "but it does surprise me that there should be so much hatred and dishonesty" (*Letters*, 2:135). Two months later he confessed to his friend Ivan Turgenev, the Russian novelist, that he still had trouble accepting the attacks on his book: "Nothing is more foolish than to claim to be misunderstood. That is nevertheless what I think" (*Conard*, 19:219).

The virulence of some of the reviews suggests that, for the spokesmen of mainstream taste, the novel's form was unsettling and its depiction of society scandalously amoral. Jules Barbey d'Aurévilly, a novelist who attacked all of Flaubert's works in the press, set the tone when he declared that *L'Education sentimentale* was a supreme example of the wretchedness and vulgarity of realism, which he defined as a school devoted to denying the existence of heroes in modern life by proclaiming "that all the cowards and dull mediocrities are every inch their worth and are even a thousand times more interesting than they." The main character, Frédéric Moreau, was for Barbey a "witless scamp, with no character" who "vegetates like a cabbage."[8] The critic Hippolyte Taine, who was a friend of Flaubert's, thought that his characters provided a striking and exact portrait of the modern middle class; if Taine was right, it may be this very resemblance that others found offensive. Referring to the attacks on the book, George Sand wrote to Flaubert that "it confirms the present confused state of people's minds all too strongly. It rubs the raw wound" (*Letters*, 2:140). In her published review, which was intended to defend Flaubert and his book, Sand mischievously suggested that the novel was a mirror placed before its readers' eyes, a mirror in which no one might recognize his own image, but in which everyone would surely recognize his neighbor's.[9]

Several contemporary critics decried what they perceived as the absence of a story or plot, calling *Sentimental Education* a string of tableaux or episodes but not a novel. For Edmond Schérer, writing in the newspaper *Le Temps,* Flaubert had failed by trying to make fiction out of the stuff of ordinary life, which is unsuitable because it consists mostly of "facts whose cause is unknown, and which will lead to nothing, idle encounters, capricious or useless actions" (*Conard*, 4:696). Several reviewers suggested that the book was less a novel than a satire, a classical genre in which vice and folly are imitated in a spirit of indignant ridicule. In satire the weak or vulgar characters and the episodic structure would not be out of place, but critics found that in *Sentimental Education* one crucial aspect of the genre was conspicuously missing: moral outrage. In contrast to the indignation of the Roman satirist Juvenal, wrote the academician Cuvillier-Fleury in the *Journal des Débats*, Flaubert seems to say to his readers and society, "Your corruption is frightful and your vices cry out for vengeance, but it's all the same to me!" (*Conard*, 4:695). In a similar vein, the literature professor Saint-René Taillandier complained in the *Revue des deux mondes* that Flaubert's cruelly comic treatment of the revolutionary clubs in 1848 shows "a disdainful indifference that is truly an insult, not to the masses in the streets, but to the human race" (*Conard*, 4:699).

George Sand defended Flaubert's book against such charges in her review, saving her own reservations about it for her letters to Flaubert. Despite the absence of an explicitly moral perspective in *Sentimental Education*, she argued, its author had "succeeded in producing a new sensation: indignation against the perversity and cowardice of human affairs, when, at certain eras, everything goes adrift at once" (*Conard*, 4:700). As for the complex and sometimes diffuse plot, she defended it as a necessary counterpart to the character of Frédéric Moreau, whose weak self, so easily influenced by others, could only exist in relation to many other characters. "Thus the scenario of the novel, which is as multiple as living reality, intersects and intertwines itself with remarkable artistry" (*Conard*, 4:701).

Although she had been eloquent in her defense of her friend's work, Sand was apparently convinced that the novel's impersonality and bleakness, so foreign to her own idealistic fiction, were failings in what was otherwise a splendid composition. In an exchange of letters during the winter of 1875–76, she took Flaubert to task for believing that he could keep his personal convictions out of his work and still capture the interest and sympathy of his readers. She felt that in *Madame Bovary* the moral meaning of the work—"a striking lesson to vanity, to ambition, to irrationality"—was clear, but that no such lesson was discernible in *L'Education*. The public had misunderstood, she agreed, but that could only be the author's fault. Trying to stand Flaubert's doctrine of impersonality on its head, she argued that her own admiration for the novel depended on the fact that she knew its author well and thus could imagine his unexpressed judgments and sympathies:

> What the reader wants, above all, is to penetrate our thought, and that is what you arrogantly deny him. He thinks you scorn and mock him. *I* understood you, because I knew you. If I'd been given your book without your name on it, I'd have thought it splendid, but strange, and I'd have asked myself whether you were immoral, skeptical, indifferent, or heartbroken . . . . Your story is inevitably a conversation between you and the reader. If you show him evil coldly, without ever showing him good, he's angry. He wonders whether he is the villain, or you. What you wanted to do, however, was to rouse him and maintain his interest; and you will never succeed if you are not roused yourself, or if you conceal your emotion so effectively that he thinks you indifferent. He's right: supreme impartiality is antihuman, and a novel must above all be human. (*Letters*, 2:228–29)

Clearly the dissolution of the familiar bonds of communication between storyteller and listener disconcerted readers in the nineteenth century, and no one was better qualified than Sand to defend the tradition of a conversation between author and reader.

Another great novelist who found *Sentimental Education* too difficult and strange to be successful as a novel was Henry James. His strictures are pithy and memorable: the novel is "elaborately and massively dreary . . . an epic without air, without wings to lift it," and reading it "is, to the finer sense, like masticating ashes and sawdust" (James, 176, 328). James objected to the fact that most of the novel is told from the point of view of its weak hero, so that its great scope is filtered through a mediocre consciousness with whom the reader can scarcely wish to communicate. Despite his condemnation, however, James felt that the very failure of *Sentimental Education* revealed something of Flaubert's greatness:

I find myself feeling for a moment longer in presence of *L'Education* how much more interesting a writer may be on occasion by the given failure than by the given success. Successes pure and simple disconnect and dismiss him; failures—though I admit they must be a bit qualified—keep him in touch and in relation. Thus it is that as the work of a "grand écrivain" *L'Education,* large, laboured, immensely "written," with beautiful passages and a general emptiness, with a kind of leak in its stored sadness, moreover, by which its moral dignity escapes—thus it is that Flaubert's ill-starred novel is a curiosity for a literary museum. (James, 329)

Sentimental Education contributed more than any other work, James concluded, to making Flaubert the "novelist's novelist."

Judged according to the novelistic standards of its day, *Sentimental Education* appeared to be a failure, or at best a perplexing half success, but its stretching of the genre's boundaries made it a work destined to fascinate writers and readers to come, especially in our own century. As Marcel Proust wrote in the second novel of his *Remembrance of Things Past,* the great work must "create its own posterity": it is the work of genius itself which, "by fertilizing the rare minds capable of understanding it, will make them increase and multiply."[10] For the generation of French novelists that followed Flaubert, *Sentimental Education* was the prototype and masterpiece of the naturalistic slice-of-life novel; the vulgarity of its characters and the disconnectedness of its episodes were justified on the grounds that they resembled real life. Emile Zola and the naturalists associated Flaubert's name with documentary realism, an aspect of his work he considered entirely secondary, and they paid correspondingly less attention to the stylistic craftsmanship on which Flaubert believed that both the beauty and truth of his fictions depended.

In the twentieth century, both novelists and critics have more often followed the lead of Henry James than that of the naturalists, praising Flaubert's masterful writing and devotion to literature rather than celebrating his fidelity to reality. Proust felt that *Sentimental Education* was Flaubert's supreme stylistic achievement, and admired what he called the "grammatical beauty" of the use of verb tenses, conjunctions, and even commas. Flaubert's use of the imperfect tense in indirect discourse, he wrote, amounted to a perceptual revolution, which "totally transforms the appearance of things and beings, like a lamp moved to a new position or one's arrival in a new house."[11]

A few comments in Franz Kafka's letters show that no writer was more crucial to him than Flaubert, no book more important than *Sentimental Education*. Soon after beginning a correspondence with Felice Bauer, to whom he was to be twice engaged but never married, he sent her a copy of the novel, explaining that it was "a book that for many years has been as dear to me as are only two or three people; whenever and wherever I open it, I am startled and succumb to it completely, and I always feel as though I were the author's spiritual son, albeit a weak and awkward one."[12] A few weeks later, he told her of a remarkable daydream: "As a child—which I was until a few years ago—I used to enjoy dreaming of reading aloud to a large, crowded hall . . . the whole of *Education sentimentale* at one sitting, for as many days and nights as it required, in French of course (oh dear, my accent!), and making the walls reverberate" (Kafka, 86).

Although the first half of the twentieth century saw *Sentimental Education* firmly placed in the canon of great nineteenth-century novels, with mainstream critics such as Albert Thibaudet analyzing its thematic and compositional richness, its reception was often closely related to the political and ideological struggles of the era. The Hungarian critic Gyorgy Lukács praised it as the most accomplished work of the "romanticism of disillusionment" in his *Theory of the Novel* (1920), but in the 1930s, after he had become a Marxist, Lukács denounced his earlier fascination with *Sentimental Education* as a form of idealism and argued that Balzac's realism came closer to the insights of historical materialism than did Flaubert's.[13] By contrast, the critic Edmund Wilson, writing from the perspective of the American anti-Stalinist left of the late 1930s, praised *Sentimental Education* for offering a nuanced social analysis that combines the socialist critique of the failings of capitalism and middle-class society with prophetic insight into the totalitarian dangers inherent in socialism. For Wilson, as for the young Lukács, the novel's greatness resides in the artistry with which it evokes disillusion: "It is the tragedy of nobody in particular, but of the poor human race itself reduced to such ineptitude, such cowardice, such commonness, such weak irresolution—arriving, with so many fine notions in its head, so many noble words on its lips, at a failure which is all the more miserable because those who have failed are hardly conscious of having done so."[14] Perhaps echoing Virginia Woolf's praise of George Eliot's *Middlemarch* as a novel "for grown-up people," Wilson argues that *Sentimental Education* can be deeply moving to readers mature enough "to have acquired a certain interest in social as distinct from personal questions" (Wilson, 113).

In recent decades much critical interest in Flaubert has concentrated not on his supposed realism or on social questions, but on the "writerly" aspects of his work dear to James and Proust. The group of French "new novelists" of the 1950s and 1960s saw his doctrine of impersonality and his preoccupation with style as distant prefigurations of their own efforts to break with conventional narration and psychology in the novel. Flaubert's unchallenged importance in the history of the novel has made his work a canonical reference for virtually all recent critics and theorists of the novel. Structuralists, who attempt to analyze narrative as a linguistic act, susceptible to grammatical decoding, and poststructuralists, who emphasize the indeterminate and problematic character of meaning in language, have found Flaubert's carefully constructed fictions to be a fertile terrain for their analyses. Jonathan Culler's *Flaubert: The Uses of Uncertainty* (1974) argues that Flaubert's narrative technique undermines or deconstructs the assumptions of certainty and meaningfulness that had undergirded earlier novels. Flaubert's refusal to express his own intentions and judgments in his novels makes them particularly suitable objects for critical practices emphasizing the workings of language rather than the ideas of writers.

It must be noted, however, that when critics use Flaubert as a test case or illustration of their approaches to narrative, they are most likely to concentrate on *Madame Bovary.* The enormous role of history in *Sentimental Education,* and its possible autobiographical dimension, make it a problematic work for formalist criticism, although several critics—among them Peter Brooks, Graham Falconer, and Stirling Haig—have followed Culler in writing effectively about the intricacy and indeterminacy of its narration.

In general, *Sentimental Education* draws more commentary from specialists on Flaubert and on the French nineteenth century than from critics interested in the form and history of the novel. Psychologically oriented critics, such as Marthe Robert, have studied the relations between Frédéric's fixation on Madame Arnoux and similar thematic material in Flaubert's early writings and correspondence in an attempt to understand the origins of his literary vocation and artistic stance. The historian Maurice Agulhon has commented on *Sentimental Education*'s documentary value,[15] while scholars of literature and history, such as Dominick LaCapra, Dolf Oehler, and Hayden White, have emphasized the interplay between the novel's form, history, ideology, and social criticism. A fertile union of the author- and history-centered approaches can be found in the analyses of Pierre Bourdieu, who argues that Flaubert's "Story of a Young Man" both reflects its author's place in society and succeeds in presenting a complex and sociologically pertinent account of French society and its transformations during the mid nineteenth century.

For all the activity of recent critics, many readers may feel that the essential debate over *Sentimental Education* was captured in a pair of remarks from two of the novelists most devoted to Flaubert's work. In January 1870, George Sand described to Flaubert how the young people staying at her house, several of whom had met him, reacted to his novel: "The youngest say that *L'Education sentimentale* made them sad. They didn't recognize themselves in it, they who haven't yet lived. But they have illusions, and they say: Why does this man, so good, so lovable, so gay, so simple, so sympathetic, want to discourage us from living? It isn't properly thought out, what they say, but since it's instinctive, it should perhaps be taken into account" (*Letters,* 2:140–41). It is fitting that the most eloquent response to this reproach should have come from Franz Kafka, whose way of living to the fullest was to give up the activities most people call life so as to devote himself body and soul to literature. In a 1913 letter to Felice Bauer, Kafka wrote of *Sentimental Education:* "What life there is in that book! If you cling to it, this life seeps into you, whoever you may be" (Kafka, 306).

20

A Reading

4

Beginnings

When readers and critics call a work *literary*, they imply (among other things) that its language and form are not disposable means of conveying ideas but are instead inextricably related to the work's content, and indeed worthy of attention in their own right. A literary work does not merely say something new; it says it in a new way. Before we read a work of literature, we do not entirely know how to read it. We may be fluent in the language in which it (or its translation) is written, and even familiar with the styles and conventions of its author, its genre, or its era, but nothing else can fully prepare us for the specific ways in which this particular text will oblige us to organize our perceptions and thoughts as we read it.

Beginnings are thus places of great strategic importance, for it is there that readers get their first and most important clues as to what is important in a work and how they should go about reading it. Themes and techniques encountered in the opening pages provide a framework for reading everything that follows, although of course that framework can be gradually—or even suddenly—altered in the course of a work. The first pages of a long novel such as *Sentimental Education* provide signposts that will help the reader move with more intelligence and less effort through the rest. A close reading of these pages, more detailed than would be possible for the book as a whole, should illuminate these signposts, and also provide ideas as to how other passages might be read attentively as well.

The novel's title—in French, *L'Education sentimentale*—strongly suggests a story of apprenticeship, initiation, or personal development. The word *éducation* refers to upbringing and training in a broad sense, not simply to what goes on in school. This distinction was even clearer in the nineteenth century, when what is now called the Education Ministry in France was known as the Ministry of Public Instruction. *Sentimentale* has the connotations of its English counterpart, but perhaps its most common meaning is "of or pertaining to love"; in this sense it would be a likely translation of *love* when asking about someone's "love life." The title thus promises a story of apprenticeship in the ways of love, with an emphasis on the tender and dreamy side of love as opposed to the passionate or the sensual.

More than any other novel by Flaubert, *Sentimental Education* belongs to the important group of nineteenth-century novels that examine the tensions between individual desire and social constraint by following the career of a young man as he sets out from home into the world and undergoes experiences that will mature him and fix his place in society. It is entirely to be expected that the first individual the reader encounters should be "a long-haired man of eighteen" who has just finished his secondary schooling. The time and place at which he is introduced, however, are less conventional. The opening paragraphs both place the novel within a nineteenth-century tradition of realist fiction and give clues as to how Flaubert's novel will assert its distinctiveness within that tradition.

The text's first indications are temporal: "On the 15th of September 1840, at six o'clock in the morning" (15). This phrase does more than give the action a certain starting point in time. Flaubert could have written "Near the end of summer a generation ago, just after dawn" without changing the referential meaning, but he chose to emphasize not the cycles of days and seasons and lives, but the recorded, measured, socially agreed upon time of calendars, clocks, and schedules.

Beginnings

Earlier novels, notably those of Balzac, often began with similar temporal indications, but these were generally less precise, especially as to the year, along the lines of, "Toward the middle of September 184*, around six o'clock," as if a certain ambiguity were necessary to provide fiction with freedom and believability by distancing it from the real. By comparison, *Sentimental Education* places itself in chronological time with assertive precision, as if to challenge historical reality on the latter's own terms. The young man of 18, when we meet him, will not be a timeless representative of adolescence, but a figure from the generation that came of age around 1840.

The subject of the novel's first sentence turns out to be a paddle wheel steamer, the *Ville-de-Montereau,* prosaically named after its port of call upriver. What is taking place at six o'clock is not a specific human action, but a mechanical process that is part of a modern, urban scene. Things, sounds, sights, and (presumably) smells predominate, and the first people mentioned are anonymous groups of passengers and sailors whose impersonal movements seem to be confounded with the disordered and growing piles of objects and the hissing steam. The novel's first scene shows people subject to characteristic processes of the early industrial age: jostled like parcels, unable to inform themselves about what is happening, they are transported upstream under steam power. The view of the banks in the third paragraph belongs to everyone and no one; it is a moving gaze produced by the boat's mechanical motion, much as the perspectives of cinema and video images are the products of technological rather than human movement. Although industry and technology are not major themes of the novel, the opening scene provides a context in which human activity, framed by technology, appears passive, confused, and impersonal.

The young man of 18, although clearly marked as an individual in whom we should take interest, is first presented anonymously, sharing the parcel-like immobility of the transported passengers and their mechanically produced view of fleeing Paris. He is differentiated only by conventional signs of an artistic, sensitive youth of the romantic era: long hair, sketchbook, sigh. The suspicion that, in this novel, objects and impersonal groupings take precedence over human individuals is reinforced when the young man is identified at the beginning of the next paragraph, for his last name turns out to be part of the steamer's name: *Montereau*.[16] Any sense of Frédéric Moreau as an autonomous or active subject is further undercut by the fact that he has been sent to Le Havre and back by his mother, with so little money that he cannot deviate from the straight route she has planned for him. So it is that the reader first encounters him engaged in an ironic action for the hero of a French novel of education: leaving Paris, instead of arriving there to make his way in the society of the capital. Because Frédéric's definitive arrival there will come only at the beginning of chapter 3, the brief opening chapters stand together as a preamble or overture to Flaubert's Parisian novel.

Following Frédéric's introduction, the next several paragraphs alternate between descriptions of the river voyage and of the young man's activities. The movement of the steamer places the same sights before the eyes of all the passengers, whose conventional socializing is described in indefinite and impersonal phrases. Seeing the houses on the river's banks, passengers fantasize about the objects of their desire, whether material or erotic. Although he considers himself distinguished by a beautiful, sensitive soul, Frédéric thinks about a parallel series of objects of desire, and this equivalence between himself and his anonymous traveling companions undercuts his sense of aesthetic superiority. Later in the chapter, his most intimate fantasies about living with Madame Arnoux will again echo the passengers' daydreams as the steamer takes them past the houses of strangers (20–21).

Before Frédéric sees Madame Arnoux, however, he meets the man who turns out to be her husband, and the encounter with Arnoux is of no less interest than the dazzling apparition of his wife. What catches Frédéric's eye is "a gentleman flirting with a peasant-girl, and toying with the gold cross which she wore on her breast" (16). The aloof young man of vague, idealized desires is drawn to an older man who is casually and confidently expressing erotic desire in its simplest form. Arnoux's gallantry is rustic, offhand, and commonplace—quite the opposite of what we should expect from a dreamy aesthete such as Frédéric. Yet this flirtation is also interesting for its slight element of indirectness: Arnoux plays with the gold cross, an object of both economic and symbolic value located in proximity to the female body that appears to be the real object of his desire. In this sense, Arnoux's first appearance in the text provides a possible model for the pursuit of desire in *Sentimental Education*. Desire is expressed by means of a displacement or detour via contiguous material objects or accessory circumstances. A few pages later, when Frédéric wants to get invited to the Arnoux household, "He could not think of any better way than to point out the autumn tints of the landscape, adding: 'Soon it will be winter, the season of balls and dinner-parties'" (21). There is, of course, a notable difference between this remark and Arnoux's tactic with the peasant girl: in his reticence, Frédéric strays so far from his object that his point is missed, whereas the sense of the older man's gesture is unmistakable.

If Frédéric first sees in Arnoux a possible model for his own desire for women, his interest becomes even more intense once the older man appears to him as a potential initiator in the artistic and entertainment worlds of Paris. Arnoux's magazine, *L'Art Industriel,* is part of the image-making industry that has helped shape Frédéric's provincial dream of Paris as the center of taste and modernity, the only place where a superior soul such as his could seek happiness. Although Frédéric's most obvious reason for frequenting Arnoux's shop and office will be his passion for Madame Arnoux, this first encounter makes clear that her husband fascinates him in his own right. In thinking about Frédéric's motives, the reader will hardly be able to separate his romantic love from his desire to know and enter the Parisian art world.

The beginning of that love, Frédéric's first sight of Madame Arnoux, is set off by a sudden and dramatic introduction, "It was like a vision:" (18). The short paragraph and the colon are specifically *textual* effects, belonging to the repertoire of the writer rather than the story-teller, the author rather than the narrator, and they startle the reader the way the woman's unexpected and dazzling apparition startle Frédéric. This introduction reminds us that we are reading fiction at the very moment when that fiction calls on us most seductively to identify with its hero's rapture. The descriptions of Madame Arnoux are presented as what Frédéric notices as he looks at her, whether frankly or while pretending to look elsewhere. Each time he examines her, his gaze seems to move outward, from her face to her hair to her dress to her embroidery and workbasket. By the time he looks at the latter object "with eyes full of wonder, as if it were something out of the ordinary," however, the text's perspective no longer coincides with that of Frédéric, who presumably is not feeling himself to be deluded regarding the basket's extraordinariness. The narrative first creates the effect of presenting its character's unmediated perceptions and then, without warning, slips into a mode of ironic distance and superiority.

The next sentences seem to come back to Frédéric's perceptions and thoughts, but this return merely provides a new occasion for readers to exercise their skeptical judgment of the form taken by his desire: "He longed to know the furniture in her room, all the dresses she had ever worn, the people she mixed with; and even the desire for physical possession gave way to a profounder yearning, a poignant curiosity which knew no bounds" (18). Here is a deflection of sexual desire toward accessory objects that goes far beyond the model of Arnoux fondling the peasant girl's cross, for rather than providing even an imaginary pretext for physical contact, Frédéric's thoughts amount first to a dispersal or scattering of his desire and finally to desire's metamorphosis into a passion for exhaustive knowledge. This form of desire is the perversion not only of Frédéric but of readers of realist fiction, who have no hope of making love to the characters they encounter but who have every reasonable expectation of finding out about their furniture, their clothes, and their acquaintances. Frédéric is fascinated by Madame Arnoux as by the heroine of a novel; his desire, in other words, is mediated or given form by realist fiction, with its conventions of evoking human characters through description of the things and social relations by which they are surrounded.

Throughout the first chapter, as Frédéric observes Madame Arnoux and dreams of her, his sudden passion is associated with literature and tinged with romantic exoticism. Her black servant suggests to him that she may be a Creole, a woman of European descent raised on a tropical island, like the heroines of novels such as George Sand's *Indiana* (1832) and Balzac's *The Girl with the Golden Eyes* (1835). Because of her presence, he feels deeply moved by an Oriental romance sung to the accompaniment of the throbbing steam engine. Watching her read a book, he feels jealous of the author who is occupying her attention. And when he reviews his impressions of her during his ride from Montereau to Nogent, he likens her to "the women in romantic novels" (22).

The most striking moment of the chapter may be one about which the narrator says not a word: Frédéric's discovery, shared by the reader, that the woman of his vision is Arnoux's wife. What are we as readers to make of the absence of any explicit reaction by Frédéric to this revelation? That he is too stunned to do anything but take refuge in the details and sensations of the voyage? Too lovestruck to care? Or, perhaps, that he is sufficiently familiar with the plots of romantic novels to know that adulterous passion often creates relations of imitation and complicity (as well as rivalry) between the lover and the husband, and thus that he welcomes the chance to associate with both Monsieur and Madame Arnoux? However we choose to fill in the blank of Frédéric's reaction to Arnoux's appearance in the role of husband, it remains a striking example of a narrative technique that lets the reader experience the same surprise as the hero. Rather than describing or explaining the event, the narrator in effect simulates it for the reader.

Only later in the chapter are we given some indication of how Frédéric sees the Arnoux couple in light of his passion. Riding homeward, he decides to become "a friend of the family" (22). Frédéric is taking reality into account in his thinking, reconciling his liking for Arnoux, his desire for his wife, and his interest in the Parisian art world he associates with both of them. He is in effect compromising with his desire, planning to pursue the more accessible goal of making his way in an artistic milieu, and hoping that success in love may follow. The reasonableness of this compromise is belied, however, by Frédéric's physical excitement, which makes him drive the horses too hard. His intermittent thoughts of Madame Arnoux contrast with the mundane events of the chapter's last pages, from the ride home to the conversation with his mother about his prospects for an inheritance from his uncle.

Frédéric's arrival in Nogent provides the occasion for giving the reader the information about family and finance characteristic of nineteenth-century realist fiction. Madame Moreau is of noble birth, respectable and respected, but she struggles in the face of a declining fortune to keep up appearances for the local worthies who admire her and frequent her drawing room. Provincial town society is depicted as fostering thrift, social conservatism, gossip, respectability, and a somewhat simplistic curiosity about national (and therefore Parisian) events. The drabness of this milieu helps explain why, to a sensitive and cultivated young man such as Frédéric, no worthwhile destiny could exist outside of Paris, and also why an opening chapter that begins in Paris but ends in Nogent is such a negative signal concerning the young man's prospects in his worldly and sentimental education.

The arrival of Frédéric's friend Charles Deslauriers provides a transition to chapter 2. His family background and social situation are evoked in at least as great detail as those of Frédéric, which suggests that the education of the novel's title may not be that of a single hero but of at least two important characters. Flaubert's first *Sentimental Education,* written between 1843 and 1845, had alternated between the lives of two young friends, Henry and Jules, and some indications of similar structure are found in the 1869 novel. Frédéric and Deslauriers form a couple: inseparable at school, they are characterized by a series of complementary contrasts. One is from the upper middle class, dominated by his mother, soft, inclined to literature and dreaming of love; the other is from the lower middle class, dominated by his father, hard, inclined to philosophy and dreaming of power. Each derives satisfaction from the chance for close friendship with one so different from himself. Frédéric's affection was born of admiration for the older boy's furious reaction to an insult to his social standing. His solidarity with Deslauriers's class resentment is based not on experience or even deep empathy, but rather on the liberating excitement of a violent riposte.

Three years apart in age, Frédéric and Deslauriers belong to the generation born following Napoleon's defeat at Waterloo and the restoration of the Bourbon monarchy, a period of economic, political, and social stagnation in France. Napoleon's Empire, although authoritarian and militaristic, was described (and probably experienced) by many as a time of opportunity, adventure, and patriotic fervor, a time when men of modest origins, like old Deslauriers and Monsieur Moreau, could win honor, and perhaps even fame and fortune, on the battlefield or in the administrative service of the expansionist state. After 1815, however, the Restoration pensioned old soldiers at half-pay, turned many administrative and diplomatic posts over to once-exiled noblemen and their allies, and in general seemed to provide a diminished—or at least politically restricted—sphere of activity for men of the middle classes. In keeping with this conventional portrayal of those years, the fictional fathers of the next generation are often either dead, like Monsieur Moreau, or underemployed and embittered, like Captain Deslauriers. In *Les Forces perdues* (Wasted Strength), a novel published two years before *L'Education sentimentale*, Flaubert's friend Maxime Du Camp attempted to diagnose the collective malaise of those born around 1820, and he insisted on the importance of a generation of fathers bereft of their emperor and their activity: "All the men of that generation bore, during their entire life, something sad and weighty, as if their fathers had passed on to them the melancholy and the humiliation that the double ruin of their hopes and their country had imposed on them."[17] Frédéric's father is not explicitly identified as a veteran of the Napoleonic wars, but his plebeian origins, his social-climbing marriage, and his early death from a sword wound place him symbolically among the men for whom the Restoration signified the stifling of dreams after the glory years of the Empire.

The contrasting intellectual interests of the two friends should be understood in relation to their differing social position. Frédéric first admired plays and memoirs from the Middle Ages, and now favors works of romantic literature that celebrate and analyze extreme passion. His preferences follow and summarize the tastes of the era in which he was raised and also identify him with forms of romanticism that are essentially aristocratic, the nostalgic and world-weary expressions of an elite that sees itself less and less as having a worthy role to play in the contemporary world. Deslauriers, on the other hand, devotes himself to writings characteristic of those progressive elements of the middle classes who, beginning in the eighteenth century, had hastened the downfall of the old social and religious order. He first studied philosophy, which in the nineteenth century was inevitably identified with the intellectual critiques of religion and social privilege advanced by the *philosophes* of the Enlightenment prior to the French Revolution. Deslauriers follows his metaphysical studies by turning to the Revolution's orators and political writers, and to Frédéric he prophesies a coming social upheaval comparable to that of 1789. His are the tastes of a social group that feels itself capable of throwing off the prejudices and traditions weighing it down and claiming its share of power and material success. The friendship of the two young men, while sincere, is based on misconceptions: Frédéric idealizes Deslauriers's fairly commonplace ambition, making the captain's son into a purer intellectual than he really is, while the law clerk assumes that the wealthy young student's literary and amorous dreams are really a form of ambition not unlike his own.

Like the first chapter, in which Frédéric's longing for Madame Arnoux interrupts the details of his return to his mother's home, the second closes with a series of contrasts between the dreams of the two friends and the real circumstances of their late-evening visit in Nogent. While they lament the obstacles that will postpone their long-awaited life together in Paris, Madame Moreau's old servant badgers Frédéric to come home at a decent hour. Monsieur Roque, a not-quite-respectable man of means who has already been discussed in the Moreau drawing room, intrudes as Frédéric intones a romantic complaint on the impossibility of love and artistic inspiration. The ever practical Deslauriers, however, sees this chance meeting not as a vulgar counterpoint to idealistic dreaming, but as an occasion to be exploited in the service of ambition: he suggests using old Roque to gain an introduction to the Parisian banker Dambreuse and thus to the world of money and power. Deslauriers here reveals himself to be an earnest if naïve reader of Balzac, urging his friend to imitate the character Rastignac (who appears in *Old Goriot* and many other novels) and become the lover of Madame Dambreuse so as to rise in the world with the help of her husband. This plan is not too different from Frédéric's own ideas about the Arnoux couple, and for the moment he seems to view the conquest of Madame Dambreuse as if it were merely another version of winning Madame Arnoux's love. Indeed, the next chapter will begin with Frédéric about to pay "his momentous call"—a visit not to Arnoux but to Dambreuse.

Chapter 2 concludes with an enigmatic reference to an escapade that will be explained only in the novel's final lines. Three years earlier,

Beginnings

Madame Moreau suspected Deslauriers of taking her son to "places of ill repute," and in response to the old coachman's plea that Frédéric return home, the clerk assures him that "he'll sleep at home tonight" (27, 29). As the two friends are about to part, a house by the river reminds them of a shared adventure involving Venus, Poverty, and Continence, and they laugh merrily together. Nothing indicates that this episode is anything but an illustration of their complicitous adolescent camaraderie or that it will ever come up again in the novel. In this sense it is emblematic of the problem of reading and interpreting details in realist fiction: some apparently trivial events and objects turn out to be highly significant, while others simply contribute to a general impression that we are reading a story about a concrete and complex world.

It is characteristic of Flaubert's narrative technique—as opposed to that of Balzac, for instance—that we are almost never told explicitly what is important and what is not. Thus any commentary on a beginning, such as the one proposed here, is inevitably shaped by knowledge of what follows and depends on the experience of rereading. Ford Madox Ford once remarked that those who had not read *Sentimental Education* at least 14 times could not really consider themselves educated. Perhaps one purpose of a study such as this one is to offer something of that experience of rereading at less cost in time to one's life.

5

Frédéric Moreau

Henry James is probably the most famous of the many readers of *Sentimental Education* who have felt frustrated by the weakness and blandness of its hero. Calling Frédéric an "abject human specimen" who leads an impoverished life, James wondered how Flaubert could not have realized that the reader, faced with the task of being interested in this young man's existence for hundreds of pages, would cry out in protest "Why, why *him?*" (James, 326–27). Regarding Frédéric as "positively too poor for his part," James judged the use of him as the main character to have been a major error, one which all but ruined the novel. If we wish to argue that James was too hard on *Sentimental Education,* that he missed something crucial in condemning the novel because of its hero's weakness, we must nonetheless take that weakness into account, for it cannot be denied or explained away. Edmund Wilson, who admired the novel greatly, wrote that Frédéric "has no stability of purpose and is capable of no emotional integrity" (Wilson, 109).

Of course, only by voluntary participation in an illusion can we speak of novelistic characters as beings possessing psychological traits such as stability of purpose; we read the novel's printed words *as if* they referred to a person named Frédéric Moreau. In reality, we have only sentences that purport to describe a person called Frédéric, his actions and his world, and these sentences are part of a literary composition we call a novel. Our participation in the illusion that Frédéric is a person is a very important part of our reading of that novel, but it need not be the only way in which we consider the work. In other words, we must take seriously the problems posed by Frédéric Moreau as a real human character, but also consider the ways in which his very failure to be readable on this level contribute to an understanding of *Sentimental Education,* which is a work of art not wholly reducible to the *story* of a group of young men starting out in life in the Paris of the 1840s.

As noted in chapter 3 herein, George Sand told Flaubert that young readers were saddened by his novel, distressed that its author seemed to want to discourage them from living. Much of the tone noted by Sand's young friends stems directly from the main character, whose passivity and indecisiveness has discouraged young readers, modern readers, and perhaps—in one way or another—all readers. There are, of course, many weak, passive, or unadmirable antiheroes in twentieth-century literary works (their most obvious prototype being the Underground Man of Dostoevsky's *Notes from the Underground*), but the nineteenth-century novel, especially the novel of initiation and education, seems to be a form difficult to sustain without a more impressive or engaging hero.

In referring to Frédéric's weakness we can usefully distinguish between his moral shallowness and his failure to grasp what life has to offer. After all, novels have plenty of amoral or even wicked characters who are full of energy and will, as well as characters of great purity and goodness who cannot or will not take pleasure or power for themselves. To many nineteenth-century readers especially, the absence of moral fibre was perhaps the most disconcerting trait of Frédéric Moreau's character. Because literary histories of the nineteenth-century novel emphasize the triumph of realism and naturalism, we often forget that realism was by no means the genre's only or even most accepted aesthetic principle. Much fiction of the period, such as Hugo's *Les Misérables* and the novels of George Sand, attempted to present heroes who were not realistic but who embodied a moral ideal, who were worthy of attention not because they were like real people but because they were better than most real people and could thus provide readers with an uplifting example.[18] Frédéric is no George Sand hero, but this is less a problem now than it was when *Sentimental Education* appeared; on the contrary, the goodness and sublimity of many of Sand's leading characters often seem archaic to contemporary readers, accustomed as they are to realism and its modernist avatars. Frédéric is not evil; indeed, he is presented as a sensitive, cultivated man capable of refined feelings, but he never exercises these qualities in a moral way, never makes a decision based on principles higher than those of convenience, complacency, and self-interest. Not only idealized goodness but any moral depth or tension seem absent from the novel.

The very absence of a moral dimension may of course be taken as a realistic achievement in portraying a world in which morality has receded as a principle of action. Yet Frédéric also seems an unsatisfactory actor in such a world. If he is no Sand hero, he is no Balzac hero either: he is not a man of energy, ambition, will, and calculation struggling mightily to win the rewards that society offers. Deslauriers, not Frédéric, brings up the model of Balzac's Rastignac, who at the end of *Old Goriot* looks down on Paris from Goriot's grave and challenges its society to a duel in which he will fight for wealth and status. Standing in the same cemetery and admiring the same view at Monsieur Dambreuse's funeral in *Sentimental Education*, Frédéric feels nothing—a remarkable and doubtless deliberate contrast with one of the most famous moments in Balzac's work (377). Unlike Deslauriers, who is always scheming to acquire power and expressing frustration that his means are so poor, Frédéric seems to wait passively for fortune and love to come to him; as he tells his mother, he wishes to go to Paris, do nothing, and become a government minister (107). Their casual friend Martinon provides another sort of contrast in this regard: hardly a man of great energy or intelligence, less refined than Frédéric in manner and sensibility, Martinon quietly and ploddingly accomplishes everything that society asks of him, inexorably rising to a position of prominence as a senator of the Second Empire.

In a revealing passage in part 1, chapter 3, Frédéric complains of his empty life in Paris to Martinon, who is actively studying law and has taken a simple working woman as his mistress. "Since Frédéric's distress had no rational cause, and since he could not ascribe it to any actual misfortune, Martinon utterly failed to understand his lamentations about life" (34). Martinon's failure to understand may be an indication of his limited sensibility, but he does point to an important aspect of Frédéric's malaise: the abstract and imaginary character of its causes. Frédéric would not want Martinon's happiness because it is too commonplace, too much in conformity with social norms and with literary clichés about the pleasures of student life and humble mistresses. Martinon has no inclination to distance himself from middle-class norms and so cannot conceive of Frédéric's alienation, which is largely based on an almost indefinable sense of distinction.

The reader's exasperation with Frédéric will presumably not be the same as that of the insensitive Martinon. A sense of distinction, or a distance from conventional norms, contributes to the interest of many a novelistic hero, for it enables the character to incarnate a conflict between the actual social order and some real or imagined alternative. The problem with Frédéric is that no such alternative emerges: he neither adopts conventional beliefs and modes of action nor possesses any strong and self-coherent position of his own to set against the world of the Martinons. The reader, who may expect a clash of values, a struggle between the ideal and the real, gets only a vague and diffuse negation, a strangely passive refusal of conventional life. We can understand that Frédéric is at odds with a vulgar and acquisitive society, but for what? Examined closely, he seems to have within him nothing better than what he rejects.

One can object, of course, that Frédéric's ideal is that of romantic love, that his passion for Madame Arnoux is the ideal for whose sake he lets ordinary pleasures and possibilities slip through his fingers. The problem here is again that he succeeds in neither a real nor an ideal sense. He does not manage to turn the ideal love into a real love, as common opinion would have him do, but he also fails to achieve any aesthetic or spiritual transcendence from contemplating and cultivating his ideal. Given the fact that his sublimated, idealized passion does not bring satisfaction in itself, Frédéric can only hope to become Madame Arnoux's lover in the vulgar manner—even as time and again he rejects the vulgarity of taking such a step. The reader is likely to agree with Deslauriers that Frédéric should either "get on with it" or "forget about it" (66).

Unwilling or unable to take his friend's advice, Frédéric imagines the delicacy and deference with which he loves Madame Arnoux to be a sign of his own refinement and superior soul. Bothered by Deslauriers's success in picking up a girl on the street and spending the night with her, he reassures himself by thinking, "As if I hadn't a love of my own, a hundred times purer, nobler, and stronger!" (85). Even before he meets Madame Arnoux, Frédéric feels himself to possess an inner distinction that entitles him to special rewards in life: "He considered that the happiness which his nobility of soul deserved was slow in coming" (16). He attempts to cultivate this feeling of inward nobility through his literary and artistic pretensions, and particularly his devotion to the lost world of the Middle Ages and to romantic literary works, which exalt passionate attachments that transcend society's humdrum rules and interests. Madame Arnoux, to him, is an incarnation of the heroines of novels, so that in loving her he identifies himself with the nobility of their heroes and the sensitivity of their authors.

The phenomenon of the *belle âme* or "beautiful soul," the person who believes that he or she is capable of more authentic or refined feeling than others, is a leitmotif of the modern era. It is a pose or strategy of the modern, atomized, doubting self, which belongs to a society defined more by competition between individuals than by a strong sense of community. One of the major literary prototypes of the beautiful soul is Alceste, the principal character of Molière's *The Misanthrope* (1666). Alceste is a nobleman who sees in the words and actions of everyone else only falsehood and flattery. He alone is honest and always says what he thinks—with results that are disastrous. To Molière's seventeenth-century audience, Alceste was comic because his overblown sense of difference and self-worth was a violation of social norms, which depended on a dose of hypocrisy and complacency so that people could get along with one another. However, as the type of the beautiful or honest soul became an increasingly attractive ideal in the face of manners and customs perceived as intolerably archaic and false or disruptively modern and vulgar, Alceste came to be seen as a more attractive figure, a superior man tragically misunderstood. For Jean-Jacques Rousseau (1712–78), Alceste was the prototype of the good and virtuous man who takes on the thankless task of reforming his fellows and their society, and Molière was an immoral playwright for having mocked him. Rousseau's own novel, *Julie or The New Heloïse,* is populated with beautiful souls who form a little society apart from the crassness and evil of the world, and his influential autobiography, *The Confessions,* tells the story of an innately good and honest self corrupted by society and yet always able to maintain a sense of integrity and superiority.

The romantic novels favored by Frédéric share this schema, to which they add an emphasis on melancholy and early death: Goethe's Werther, Chateaubriand's René, Byron's Lara, and Sand's Lélia are beautiful souls condemned to suffering in the world. The generation of Frédéric (and of Flaubert) grew up with these figures as its most prestigious and compelling literary types. The romantic agony of the sensitive and the superior was, by the late 1830s, an established and even shopworn topic, and provided an inevitable literary model onto which sensitive and artistic members of the younger generation would project their own feelings of alienation.

Yet no generation wants to experience its own predicament solely in cultural trappings borrowed from its predecessor. The attitude of Flaubert's generation toward the romanticism of the previous decades was ambivalent, combining admiration and exasperation. It could reasonably be compared to the way in which many of today's students view the culture and events of the late 1960s: fascination with what the previous generation had done, criticism of its illusions and naïveties, and resentment that little opportunity seems to arise for their own generation to experience something comparable yet different. Through the figure of Frédéric, Flaubert's novel participates in, but also condemns, the romanticism of passion and melancholy.

Frédéric's weakness of character is necessary to the novel's critique of the romanticism of beautiful and passionate souls. The heroes and heroines of the books he admires are presented as admirably and authentically sensitive; the readers of these books tend to believe that they are reading about beautiful souls. The readers are thus seduced into participating in the very illusion of singularity and superiority that constitutes the existence of the "beautiful soul." Readers may deplore Werther's suicide or Lélia's early death, but in the main their sympathies are with the suffering hero or heroine, their resentment is against the society in which these lofty figures cannot live. Because Frédéric, by contrast, is ultimately so ordinary, so much to blame for his own troubles, readers of *Sentimental Education* must come to terms with the illusory character of his—and perhaps anyone's—"nobility of soul." Were Frédéric a more attractive figure, or his grand passion for Madame Arnoux more clearly a source of transcendent inner happiness to him, we would be tempted to believe that his way of life was exemplary and that society should have done better by him. As it stands, the reader is invited to condemn the kind of attitude and emotion that leads him to fritter away his existence.

The romantic sensibility that Frédéric admires—and imitatively incarnates—also has an important social dimension. The nobility of soul he feels in himself is linked to an uneasy sense of class superiority, just as French romanticism was inaugurated by writers who came from the displaced upper classes in the years following the French Revolution. In exalting nature, passion, and nostalgia for the past, the romantics articulated a symbolic protest against present-day conditions of life, in which they experienced society, rationality, and change as forms of constraint inhibiting individual fulfillment. The Revolution of 1789–99 and the successive changes of regime that followed—the Consulate and Empire through 1815, then the Bourbon Restoration through 1830, then the July Monarchy born in place of a miscarried republican revolution—made the early nineteenth century in France an era in which each generation experienced fundamental changes in the principles by which society was organized and in the forms of activity expected of individuals. Each generation had to discover a social reality that, because of rapid change, did not correspond to expectations formed in its early years. Above all, perhaps, the postrevolutionary half-century was a period in which money was increasingly perceived as a fundamental social constraint. The practices and values of the middle classes became those of society at large, so that competition between individuals based on wealth and/or productivity displaced earlier forms of social relation dependent on membership in groups such as families, trades, professions, religious orders, and social classes.

These transformations were most acutely perceived by those who were threatened by them and whose culture and leisure enabled them to contemplate and describe their situation: members of elevated social strata whose privileges and way of life were put at risk by change. This is the milieu of romanticism, and it is also that of the romantics' epigone Frédéric Moreau. A German sociologist of manners, Norbert Elias, has proposed that romanticism be understood not as a literary and artistic movement of the early nineteenth century but rather as a transhistorical social phenomenon, a symbolic reaction of elites when change and new forms of social constraint threaten their way of life.[19] Unlike have-nots, who can see opportunity in unsettling change and who can react to worsened conditions of life with revolt or revolution, since they have much to gain and little to lose, elites cannot generally afford to contest the social order radically, even if they feel it to be increasingly confining or distasteful, for whatever privileged position they still possess depends on the continued existence of that order. They are thus tempted to seek imaginary or symbolic consolations in nostalgia for a past that becomes a golden age, a life lived more spontaneously and closer to nature, in which passion and pleasure are less subject to the artificial dictates of manners or the calculated necessities of competition.

Frédéric's sense of his nobility of soul, and his melancholy and passive attitude toward his situation, cannot be divorced from his sense of social distinction. As he walks among the crowds on the Paris boulevards, we are invited first to share his sensitive reaction to the coarseness of the masses, and then to realize the fatuousness of his own pretensions at superiority: "He felt utterly nauseated by the vulgarity of their faces, the stupidity of their talk, and the imbecile satisfaction glistening on their sweating brows. However, the knowledge that he was worth more than these men lessened the fatigue of looking at them" (75).

The desire to live elegantly, do nothing, and become a cabinet minister is a sign of Frédéric's romantic adoption of an aristocratic persona. To the court nobility of the Old Regime, the refined cultivation of civilized pleasures and social graces was a good in itself, as well as an important confirmation of social distinction. Commerce and most professions, by contrast, were seen as unworthy of a gentleman, and the most socially acceptable paid positions were those in the service of the sovereign. When Frédéric inherits his uncle's fortune, he desires neither to invest it so as to become wealthier, in the manner of Monsieur Dambreuse, nor to use it to win political or artistic influence, as Deslauriers and Hussonnet would have him do, but instead to lead the life of an idle young gentleman, cultivating worldly relations that will eventually lead him to a prestigious and powerful post.

Through Frédéric's sense of taste and distinction, readers of *Sentimental Education* perceive the vulgarity and venality of mid-nineteenth-century bourgeois society in its several variants, the milieus of Arnoux, Dambreuse, Roque, Martinon, and Deslauriers. All are competitive, acquisitive individuals whose selfishness offends the "beautiful soul," and in this sense Frédéric's disengagement from their activities amounts to yet another romantic critique of bourgeois society. But the *belle âme* is no less a representative of rampant individualism than the selfish bourgeois. Through his pseudo-aristocratic lifestyle, Frédéric makes a gesture of indirect (and ineffectual) opposition to bourgeois life organized around the principle of acquisitive individual ambition, but his lifestyle is itself a part of that life and a symptom of its individualism. His inability to transcend—even in his own imagination—the shoddiness and selfishness around him makes Frédéric embody the contradiction at the heart of the romantic protest against bourgeois society, and makes his failure an illustration of that protest's ineffectiveness.

The strangest and (to many readers) most frustrating of Frédéric's traits is probably his timidity, or more precisely the almost unbelievable indirectness with which he pursues his desire. As noted in chapter 4 herein, his passion for Madame Arnoux initially makes him curious about her furniture, clothes, and acquaintances, so that his desire can be said to imitate that of readers of realist fiction. Even when he first sees her, his gaze transforms her into a series of objects moving outward from her eyes: hat, ribbons, hair, dress, embroidery. His capacity to convert his passion into a desire for objects has no limits. The name

Arnoux on the sign at *L'Art Industriel* becomes like a "sacred script" to him, and he gazes with longing and fascination at the windows above the shop, even describing them in the fantasy novel he begins to write about his passion. When he learns that in fact she and Arnoux live elsewhere, the shop and its contents lose their interest for him, but when he is invited to their home the objects around her become for him "as important as works of art . . . they all took possession of his heart and strengthened his passion" (66).

In part 2, it is in large part through Frédéric's fetishization of objects that we see his passion for Madame Arnoux simultaneously developing and unraveling. When he finds her living in a new apartment, without many of the objects he had formerly associated with her, his desire is diminished, as if he is unable to transfer back to her all the feeling he had invested in the things around her. Yet soon he is reinvesting his passion in a new set of objects: the pottery dishes and statuettes manufactured and traded by Arnoux. He discovers that the pottery is a major item in the promiscuous circulation of objects back and forth between the Arnoux household and that of Rosanette, Arnoux's mistress. At her masked ball, where he has recognized with anguish the chandelier of the old *L'Art Industriel* shop, the guests smash the pottery plates from Arnoux and throw them around the room, as if mocking and scattering Frédéric's tender and timid passion. Despite (or perhaps because of) this scene of degradation, he soon buys "two flower-stands from Arnoux's shop" for his new mansion (134). Visiting Madame Arnoux at the pottery factory, he tells her that he regrets not being in the pottery industry himself, so as to be near her, and he asks to keep a little piece of paste on which she has pressed her hand.

No less important than the myriad displacements by which Frédéric's desire becomes a fetishistic desire of objects is the role of money and exchange in his pursuit of them. Worried that Madame Arnoux may be dead because he has seen her husband at the theater with two other women, he buys an engraving at *L'Art Industriel* so as to ask about her, as if he could not accomplish this simple social task without securing his right to be in the shop by a purchase. It is as if he fears he would have no social existence without spending his money. He is obsessed with buying Madame Arnoux an expensive parasol to replace the one he broke, which he thinks was hers although it presumably belonged to a passing mistress of Arnoux. He buys used pottery plates. His desire, which is a desire for an abstraction more than a desire for a person, becomes a vague force that makes objects valuable to him and makes him want to purchase them. Madame Arnoux, or rather Frédéric's image of her, functions for him as advertising images do for the modern consumer, although in a more extreme and obsessive manner: "As he walked past the shops, he looked at the cashmeres, the laces, and the jewelled ear-drops, imagining them draped about her waist, sewn on her corsage, or gleaming in her black hair. In the flowergirls' baskets, the blossoms opened for her to choose them as she passed; in the shoemakers' window, the little satin slippers edged with swansdown seemed to be waiting for her feet" (78). The comparison to twentieth-century advertising is hardly farfetched if we recall that Madame Arnoux is for Frédéric a vehicle onto which he projects fantasies derived from his experience of the mass-produced entertainment of his time ("She looked like the women in romantic novels"). Frédéric's "fetishism of commodities" is thus not that of Marx (who originated the phrase to designate the social relation between the labor of different individuals that is dissimulated in commodities as a relation between things) but that of the modern consumer, for whom the value of things made and sold is largely created by the cultural practices of the mass media and advertising.

No commodity, however, is more important to Frédéric's passion than his own money. When his mother tells him that he is without fortune, he feels that it will be impossible to see Madame Arnoux again because his sense that he is a person worthy of frequenting her household depends upon his wealth, without which he considers himself a nobody, not even fit to live in Paris at all. He all but forgets his great love until the news of his inheritance suddenly reawakens in him the feeling that he is worthy of seeing the capital and Madame Arnoux once more. Not long after his return, he tries to impress her by mentioning his new fortune: "How could he impress her? By what means? After careful consideration, Frédéric could think of nothing better than money" (140). Given the pattern of Frédéric's reliance on wealth and purchasing power, one can only smile at "after careful consideration," whose irony is another indication of the illusory character of his feelings of distinction and nobility of soul. Frédéric may feel himself to be more refined and noble than those around him, and may thus be disappointed that he can come up with nothing better to impress Madame Arnoux, but if we have been reading carefully we know that money is what he usually thinks of first.

Frédéric's wealth, which of course provides him with his substantial freedom of choice, also forms a subtle but very compelling constraint on his actions. Because he can always acquire the goods and services that immediately come to his mind as substitutes for the real objects of his desire, he never ceases to reduce his experience of life to what money can buy. His inheritance enables him to avoid the hectic career moves of Deslauriers and Hussonnet; it opens the Dambreuse circle to him and allows him to dress and decorate with a sure (if conventional) sense of style. Yet in avoiding the vulgar pursuit of a career he also avoids accomplishing anything meaningful in his life. Except for a brief moment when he imagines himself impressing Madame Arnoux with his struggles as a poor genius in a garret, Frédéric never even thinks of getting outside the kind of commodified relationship to life that money induces. At the novel's end, the narrator can describe Frédéric —in contrast to Deslauriers, whose many activities get a paragraph— by stating what has happened to his money: he has spent two-thirds of it and is reduced to living cheaply on what remains. Wealth provides Frédéric with freedom, which he uses only to follow the path of least resistance made possible by wealth.

Fetishism of objects and excessive reliance on money are not, however, the only socially interesting manifestations of Frédéric's ineffectual character. No less interesting is his diffidence in the use of language. Time and again he tries to advance his cause with Madame Arnoux by making remarks that are so far from the point as to be incongruous or almost incomprehensible. In the opening chapter, fishing an invitation from the Arnoux couple, he points out fall colors in the trees so as to mention "the season of balls and dinner-parties" (21). A similarly convoluted detour occurs when he decides to mention the severity of his old acquaintance, Sénécal, toward a worker so as to praise kindness and suggest that Madame Arnoux should be treat his love less harshly: "But as soon as he was seated beside her he found himself in difficulties: he did not know how to begin. Luckily he thought of Sénécal" (201).

These extreme displacements of desire in its expression can be seen not only as an indication of the unreal quality of Frédéric's passion for Madame Arnoux, but also as exaggerations or parodies of the conventions of speech in middle-class society, in which it is rarely considered polite or appropriate to ask for anything too directly, especially when money or intimate feelings are concerned. Monsieur Dambreuse, for example, presumably insinuating that Frédéric is Madame Arnoux's lover, asks him, "Are you a . . . close friend of theirs?" (192). When the banker dies, his acquaintances' lack of respect for him is masked, in public at least, by flowery speeches, and Frédéric helps Madame Dambreuse conceal from her servants her joy at becoming a widow. In his relations with Madame Arnoux, he takes this kind of self-control, intended to preserve decorum and show refinement, to ludicrous extremes. One of the narrator's rare maxims underlines the connection between Frédéric's timidity and middle-class decorum: "deep feelings of affection are like respectable women; they are afraid of being found out and go through life with downcast eyes" (174). Frédéric has so perfectly and excessively adopted the manners of bourgeois society—the manners that in our own day dictate such phrases as "to pass on" and "to use the bathroom"—that they stifle him and make him unfit for that very society. He can no more escape his refinement than he can his wealth: both are bourgeois social principles that he pushes to an absurd, dysfunctional extreme.

Frédéric Moreau is not a reasonable, believable young man, and his endlessly reenacted inability to act stretches the patience of the reader of realist novels to its limit. He is instead a character who seems to have been arbitrarily assigned the role of always acting so as to maintain his distance from bourgeois life, keeping up the romantic stance of suffering superiority without having any tangible suffering or credible superiority that would justify his so doing in the reader's eyes. Because the romantic protest against modern individualism is caught in the contradiction of its own self-centeredness it can be neither lucid nor effective. The "beautiful soul" can only get along in real life by abandoning the stance of abso-

Frédéric Moreau

lute individuality, or by truly believing in some form of nostalgic or aesthetic ideal that serves as a symbolic consolation or refuge from the affronts of the everyday world. Neither solution can long be adopted by Frédéric, the incurable and unconvincing romantic. He may intermittently give up his love for Madame Arnoux, but he never makes the kind of accommodation with his ideal that would enable him to get on with his life, and he never turns it into a securely sublimated memory or ideal, a spiritual treasure by which to live. By emptying the romantic stance of spiritual or aesthetic content, and yet never freeing his character from that stance, Flaubert exposes the contradiction that is romanticism. Frédéric's inadequacy as a realistic character makes him an exemplary figure of the romantic protest's incompatibility with reality.

6

Industrial Art

Frédéric Moreau is no artist. He composes a few German waltzes and starts a few literary compositions, but never works on them seriously. When he decides that his vocation is to be a great painter, he goes so far as to buy some supplies and frequent a studio. He cannot even be called a failed artist. His first ambitions, however, are artistic in the broad sense, and in trying to understand his relation to the art world we must first understand that the desire to have the sensitivity, image, or fame of an artist is quite different from the concrete project of becoming an artist. Frédéric's pursuit of an artistic vocation is too feeble to be taken seriously, but his fascination with the *idea* of being an artist is nonetheless significant, and via Arnoux he seeks initiation into an artistic milieu. Through Arnoux and the characters Frédéric encounters around him, Flaubert presents a complex analysis of the social phenomenon of art and its degradation in the nineteenth century.

Painting is the form of art most evident in *Sentimental Education*: it was Arnoux's original vocation before being briefly Frédéric's, and the painter Pellerin is the only artist among the characters. In using the words *art* and *artist* with respect to the novel, however, we should not restrict them to painting or even to the "fine arts" in general, for the words had undergone a significant extension of their meaning in the early nineteenth century, particularly in France. An *artist,* according to an 1838 dictionary, could be either a practitioner of the fine arts or one who has a feel for the arts, or who displays, in appreciating artworks and the beauties of nature, the taste and enthusiasm of an artist. In a manifesto entitled "To Be an Artist!" in the new review *L'Artiste* (1831), the writer Jules Janin exclaimed, "Art is life, art is a gift of the soul in various forms. . . . Philosophy, history, drama, painting, what does the name matter? All that is art."[20] Art came to signify a creative sensibility common to the creators of all works of beauty and imagination and to those best able to appreciate such works.

The early nineteenth century, with its awareness of the importance of money and commerce in all spheres, was also an era in which the long-term shift from patronage to the market in the economic support of art was acutely felt and often discussed. The importance of selling literary and artistic works to whomever would buy them, as opposed to producing them for a paying patron, had increased steadily throughout the eighteenth century. The phenomenon of the market was thus not new, but after the revolutions of 1789 and 1830 it became increasingly clear that the old forms of patronage were not merely interrupted but finished, and that production for a market was henceforth virtually the only possibility. Both freedom from direct subservience to patrons and anxiety about indirect subservience to an impersonal class of potential cultural consumers contributed to a new and powerfully expressed desire for the *autonomy* of art.

Works of art, in this view, should be produced in accordance with their own laws, the traditions and forms of their genres, and should be judged by the community of artists, not by governments, academic authorities, or mere consumers. Artistic activity was understood to be ideally an exercise in freedom, the antithesis of everything routine, conformist, and calculated in the everyday world. In an 1830 article, "On Artists," Balzac argued that because art is the enemy of uniformity, one could hardly expect people preoccupied by money, pleasure, commerce, or government to judge or reward it properly, and he called on all those with creative gifts to "cultivate art for art itself."[21] The antithesis of the artist and the *bourgeois,* in which the latter is understood as the financially secure and orderly solid citizen with no appreciation for the creative or the unusual, probably arose in the 1830s in apprentice painters' circles and was a commonplace by mid century. In 1865, Flaubert complained to a correspondent that "no one, at present, is concerned with Art! with Art in itself! We're sinking, becoming bourgeois in a frightful way and I don't want to see the twentieth century. The thirtieth is a different matter!" (*Pléiade,* 3:439).

In his desire to belong to the world of art, Frédéric Moreau may therefore be expressing something quite different from a calling to a particular type of artistic *production.* Authors, theaters, literary cafés, and studios signify for him a place of self-determination, an alternative to the confining, provincial life of his mother's town and the narrow career paths that might await him there. His commitment to an artistic career is not that of the disciplined practitioner of a specific skill or talent: it is a commitment to a life of freedom, fame, and pleasure, an attempt to seek fulfillment for his "beautiful soul." The frivolity of such a vocation hardly needs emphasis, but what is painful to notice in Frédéric's literary ambition is that it is doubly, even triply, unoriginal. "The pictures which these books [medieval memoirs] conjured up in his mind haunted him so persistently that he felt an urge to copy them. He nursed an ambition to become the Walter Scott of France" (26). The ambition to create has its roots in an obsessive urge to copy, and the literary project imitates a writer famous for historical novels, many of them set during the Middle Ages. Moreover, in wanting to become the Walter Scott of France, Frédéric imitates Lucien de Rubempré of Balzac's *Lost Illusions,* who was as close to a weak character or antihero as Balzac ever created. What appears to Frédéric to be a road to freedom and autonomy is thus denounced to the reader as a compulsion to repeat the work of others.

When Frédéric tells Deslauriers that "It's powerful emotions that produce great works of art" (28), he reveals the extent to which he believes art to be essentially a means of self-fulfillment for the noble soul. His comment also places him within a romantic aesthetic of feeling and personal expression against which Flaubert railed for most of his adult life. In his first *Sentimental Education,* written from 1843 to 1845 and never published in his lifetime, Flaubert described a serious artistic apprenticeship as a painful process in which the naïve belief that art and emotion go together must be destroyed so as to be replaced by an aesthetic of dedicated craftsmanship and impersonality. For the young author Jules at the end of the first *Sentimental Education,* the freedom and autonomy of art imply giving up personal expression to serve the formal necessities of the work, whose laws are larger than any individual. Frédéric has not learned this lesson, which is characteristic of Flaubert's own aesthetic pronouncements, and indeed will never learn it.

Flaubert's condemnation of self-expression in art (by which, in his own case, he means literature) can be found in his work as early as 1839, in the dedication to his quasi-autobiographical *Mémoires d'un fou.* Here he admits that in the course of the writing his own personality broke through his literary project and became dominant: "the soul moved the pen and crushed it."[22] His doctrine of impersonality becomes a leitmotiv in his letters beginning in the mid 1840s, that is, following the completion of the first *Sentimental Education,* and his most famous and characteristic expressions of it date from the early 1850s when he was writing *Madame Bovary.* To Louise Colet he writes in March 1852:

> There is nothing weaker than to put one's personal feelings into art. Follow this axiom step by step, line by line, may it always be unshakeable in your conviction . . . and you'll see! you'll see! how your horizon will be enlarged, how your vocal organ will resound, and what serenity will fill you! Pushed out to the horizon, your heart will illuminate it from the background, instead of blinding you in the foreground. With yourself scattered in all of them, your characters will live, and instead of an eternal declamatory personality . . . crowds of humanity will be seen in your works. (*Pléiade,* 2:61)

Flaubert also claimed that art should be independent of all causes, political doctrines, and attempts to prove or teach something. He thought that the writer, in order to strive for truth and universality, ought to have no attachments to country, religion, or other social ties. Above all, perhaps, he was upset by the prospect of writing as a career, as a way of earning money. *Madame Bovary* was his first published work, so that his letters of the early 1850s present the rare phenomenon of a writer completely mature in style and artistic convictions who can justifiably claim to be untouched by the literary marketplace. Although he did earn fairly substantial sums from the sale of his novels, especially *Salammbô* and *Sentimental Education*, he took so long to write them that he never could have supported himself on his literary income, and he thus continued to consider that writing was not really a career for him in the usual sense.

Because he remains aloof from every possible determining choice in life—career, marriage, religion, or political affiliation—Frédéric Moreau's social position resembles that of Flaubert and of the artist as theorized by Flaubert. Frédéric's experiences in the art world, however, are antithetical to his creator's ideals of purity, independence, and impersonality. Far from losing his illusions about the interdependence of art and sentiment, he wallows in them. When he hears Pellerin rhapsodizing on "the purpose of art . . . which is to give us an impersonal sense of exaltation," his mounting enthusiasm comes not from the aesthetic doctrine (which, although expressed with Pellerin's usual imprecision, is close to that of Flaubert) but from his confusion of this artistic idealism with his ideal love: "Frédéric watched Madame Arnoux as he listened to these words. They sank into his mind like metals into a furnace, adding to his passion and filling him with love" (58).

Following the Arnoux dinner party at which he hears these words, Frédéric chooses an artistic vocation in a moment so ludicrous that the reader can scarcely avoid a burst of laughter. Perhaps nowhere else is the narration's ironic distance from the thoughts of Frédéric it is reporting more extreme or more deflating: "He had been endowed with an extraordinary talent, the object of which he did not know. He asked himself in all seriousness whether he was to be a great painter or a great poet; and he decided in favour of painting, for the demands of this profession would bring him closer to Madame Arnoux. So he had found his vocation!" (61). It would be more prophetic to say that he had lost his vocation, for after buying some supplies and hanging around Pellerin's studio for a while Frédéric does nothing more with painting, and only briefly takes up some new literary projects. Contrary to the expectations created when Frédéric is first presented, *Sentimental Education* is not a novel of artistic education. The art world is presented not through the hero's initiation into it but through the activities of secondary characters such as Arnoux and Pellerin, activities of no great meaning to Frédéric but simply a part of the social phenomena through which he drifts.

L'Art Industriel is initially described as a "hybrid establishment," which refers literally to its being both an art magazine and a shop, but figuratively suggests some sort of impure or unnatural combination, such as that of art and industry in its name. When Frédéric first happens upon the shop in Paris, it is described as a place where art objects, curios, catalogues, and magazines are incongruously juxtaposed. The most prominent signs at the entry are proper names (Arnoux's, of course, and the initials of other publishers) and subscription prices. Moreover, the interior has been designed to give the appearance of a drawing room, while not hiding that it is a shop. The overall impression is one of amalgamation, or a lack of distinctions: the categories of art and commerce, art and furnishings, even public and private space seem to collapse into a single undifferentiated existence.

When Frédéric is reintroduced to Arnoux by Hussonnet, and encounters for the first time the circle of artists and go-betweens who frequent *L'Art Industriel,* the description again emphasizes the vague character of the place by calling it "a neutral territory where rival factions could rub shoulders" (45). It is worth noting that another social space in the novel will be described in virtually the same terms: after the 1848 revolution, "courtesans' drawing-rooms . . . served as neutral territory on which reactionaries of different parties could meet" (385). *L'Art Industriel,* where art is sold and artistic factions mingle, is thus compared to the houses where sex is sold and political deals prepared. The prostitution of art parallels the prostitution of women and of politics. The conversation at *L'Art Industriel*—and after dinner at Arnoux's—centers not on art itself but on the sex lives of models and artists and on the price of artworks. Frédéric soon learns that Arnoux is a master of shady and deceptive deals, a manipulator and corrupter of artists. He is also an artistic populist, who wants to profit by extending the field of art into the decorative and furnishing trades: "His aim was the emancipation of the arts, the sublime at a popular price. All the Paris luxury trades came under his influence, which was good in small matters, but baneful when larger issues were involved. With his passion for pandering to the public, he led able artists astray" (50). Arnoux's efforts at blurring the distinction between high art and consumer goods are said to cheapen the former, which is implicitly deemed more important than the latter. His dishonest business practices further discredit his attempts to enroll art in the service of profitable consumption.

The artists who hang out at Arnoux's shop are not as Frédéric had imagined them: his refinement and his idealistic view of art make him notice their coarseness and venality. Nonetheless, he frequents the shop assiduously, both in the hope that he will be able to spend time with Madame Arnoux and because he seems intrigued by this artistic milieu, even if it is not as pure as he had expected. It is another case of Frédéric's almost infinite capacity for accepting substitutions and displacements: failing to find the transcendent, disinterested geniuses he had hoped to meet in the art world, he is willing to spend his time with the rather unimpressive lot he has found in their place. Moreover, Arnoux's society includes one figure, Pellerin, who seems to correspond to the passionate and independent artistic type Frédéric had dreamed of and hoped to imitate.

Pellerin's first appearance comes during Frédéric's first visit to the *L'Art Industriel* circle, when the other artists are talking prices and complaining about not earning enough. Intense and slightly disheveled, looking the part of the unconventional artist, he denounces them for their mercenary chitchat: "What a bunch of shopkeepers you are!" (45). The French word translated into English as *shopkeepers* is *bourgeois,* the most general and conventional insult used in artistic circles to describe those who fail to understand or serve art on its own terms. Pellerin cites great artists of earlier eras who were not so concerned with making money, implying that the age of industrial art is also an age of artistic decadence. Soon, however, he blushes when a remark from Arnoux reveals that he is furnishing the dealer with decorative panels in the manner of Boucher, an eighteenth-century painter of mythological and pastoral scenes whose style, in the nineteenth century, would have seemed horribly dated and artistically insignificant. No person of artistic sensibility would want such panels: they can only be destined for that despised creature, the bourgeois, conventional and backward-looking. Pellerin may be the theorist of artistic autonomy and disinterestedness, but he belongs to the industrial art world and can deliver the goods when needed.

Pellerin's defense of artistic ideals does not make him a successful artist. He is far too preoccupied with the theory of art to be successful in practice, and his extensive readings in aesthetics both waste his time and confuse him. At 50 he has produced only sketches, apparently because of his conviction that without the proper theoretical understanding nothing he could paint would be great enough to be worth doing. Pellerin is too weak, or too deluded by his theories, to be bothered by his artistic failures. Visiting his studio for the first time, Frédéric sees "two large pictures, in which the first tints, scattered here and there, formed patches of brown, red, and blue on the white canvas. Over them there stretched a tracery of chalk lines, like the meshes of a net which had been mended time and again; indeed it was absolutely impossible to make anything of it" (48). In Pellerin's portrait of Rosanette's dead baby, "patches of red, yellow, green and indigo clashed in violent contrast; the thing was hideous, almost laughable" (400). Yet these failures are not tragic; they seem quite meaningless, and affect Pellerin not at all.

Laziness, misguided activity, and the gap between his ideas and his achievements leave Pellerin frustrated and inconsistent. When he paints Rosanette, and thinks that her portrait will make a great man of him, he finally imitates Renaissance painters, and in talking about them refers not to their works but to the lives of luxury they led. Because he believes himself to understand aesthetic questions better than others do, he often launches into an outburst of criticism of some institution or group: the Institute, tradesmen, the Versailles Museum under the July Monarchy, and the Second Republic. Time and again he defends the autonomy of art against Sénécal's reductive and politicized moralizing, but he wants the July Monarchy to "legislate in the interests of Art" by providing a chair in aesthetics to educate the masses, and from the Republic he requests "a sort of Stock Exchange handling aesthetic interests" (144, 294). After the 1848 revolution he paints a ludicrous political allegory showing "the Republic, or Progress, or Civilization, in the form of Christ driving a locomotive through a virgin forest" (298). When Frédéric and Deslauriers catch up on the lives of their friends in the novel's last chapter, Pellerin's varied and incoherent career is no surprise. Like Frédéric, the painter has pursued an ideal and made only ineffectual attempts to realize it.

A quite different sort of artistic pretension is found in Hussonnet, the "bohemian" who is amusing himself by speaking archaic French when Frédéric meets him on the sidelines of a demonstration. His devotion is not to art but to a lifestyle associated with artists. The terms *bohemia* and *bohemian* came into widespread use in the 1830s and 1840s in France to describe young people and would-be artists, long on talent or hope and short on achievement and cash, whose unstable and spontaneous lives seem the antithesis of bourgeois security and conventionality. Many bohemians, real or fictional, were aspiring artists and writers, but the term was often extended to those whose talent and dreams lay in other areas or who were just playing at the life of the starving artist.[23] The stories that popularized the notion of bohemia were tales of misery resourcefully staved off or gaily endured, of clever tricks played on landlords and rich uncles, of easy yet sometimes poignant love. These themes were given their most famous expression in Puccini's opera *La Bohème,* directly based on Henry Murger's *Scenes of Bohemian Life,* which was both a play (1849) and a series of stories and sketches (collected in book form in 1851). Hussonnet's "picturesque account of how he had spent an entire winter with nothing to eat but some Dutch cheese" at the Arnoux dinner party identifies him as a stereotypical bohemian in the manner of Murger's characters (57).

Unlike Pellerin and even Frédéric, Hussonnet has no desire to create ideal or moving works. He wants to enjoy himself and get ahead. He concentrates his efforts on the theater and journalism, the literary fields in which the economic rewards were the most immediate and which were the most dependent on influence and contacts in the appropriate Parisian milieu. Hussonnet needs to flaunt a bohemian manner because it is his only claim to any intellectual or artistic interest. His mask is a mythical France of bygone eras—its language, the whiskers and titles of its pleasure-loving aristocracy, its gallantry and mocking wit. Accordingly, his proclaimed taste is conservative, and above all antiromantic, since romanticism in France was often cast by its detractors as a foreign-inspired rejection of the grandeur and purity of French classicism, an Anglophilic or Germanophilic perversion of national taste. Seeing the works of Hugo and Lamartine at Frédéric's, Hussonet delivers "a sarcastic attack on the romantic school. Those poets lacked both common-sense and grammar, and above all they were not French!" (44).

Hussonnet's antiromantic stance leaves him with little to stand for artistically except eccentricity; at Frédéric's housewarming he opines that "such-and-such a folk song had more poetry in it than all the lyrics of the nineteenth century" (146). For him the world of arts and letters consists above all in personal relations, odd jobs, and spicy anecdotes. He becomes a hired pen, adopting whatever opinion he is paid to express or that he thinks will sell. His facile habit of posing as an original wit by denying or attacking everything conventional makes his conversation both obvious and irritating, especially to a sensitive and cultivated person such as Frédéric. The one consistent factor in his preferences is their politically conservative character: he enters the Dambreuse circle as the "spokesman for a reactionary club" and writes a campaign biography of the reactionary industrialist Fumichon. Under the Second Empire he becomes a high government official, watching over the press and the theaters. Rather than defending the autonomy of culture, Hussonnet uses cultural life as the lever of his ambition and ends up as chief censor.

Even less admirable than Hussonnet, and certainly further from Frédéric and thus from the novel's central perspective, is the singer and actor Delmar, the object of a jealous rivalry between Rosanette and the unflatteringly depicted bluestocking, Mademoiselle Vatnaz. He is portrayed as vulgar and vain, given to vaunting his talents and using impressive words that he does not understand. His artistic destiny, as it turns out, is to be typecast as a spokesman of the people and a prophet of revolution: "his occupation now consisted in insulting the monarchs of every country under the sun" (177–78). Confusing the actor with the role, the fans of these political plays worship him as a saint or a Messiah; Mademoiselle Vatnaz tells Frédéric that Delmar has a "humanitarian soul" and that he understands "the priestly role of the artist" (256). Like Pellerin, he goes to the *Club de l'Intelligence* after the 1848 revolution to try his hand at political candidacy. Delmar's role in the novel is apparently to illustrate not only the degradation of art by politics but also the complicity between revolutionary fervor and sentimental religiosity—a frequent theme of Flaubert's letters during the composition of *Sentimental Education*.[24]

A character as flatly and fragmentarily portrayed as Delmar holds scarcely more interest than an inanimate object—and many objects in the novel are virtual characters in their own right, from Madame Arnoux's shawl to her silver letter box, to say nothing of the pottery that fascinates Frédéric because of its association with her husband. *Sentimental Education* has no major works of art, but curios, furnishings, and decorations are crucial to the novel's analysis of the fate of art in the age of industry. The nineteenth-century middle classes, according to Flaubert's novel, mix styles and confuse art objects with all sorts of other decorations. Arnoux's downward series of career changes—from artist to art dealer to pottery manufacturer to seller of religious articles—encourages the reader to see this confusion of styles and genres as part of a story of artistic decadence.

Trying to convince Frédéric to help him take over a newspaper, Deslauriers compares the ingredients of sentimental utopias to a hodge-podge of styles in a redecorating project: "this magnificent, much admired society, made up of Louis Quatorze relics and Voltairian ruins with a coat of Imperial paint and fragments of the English constitution . . ." (180). He could be speaking about any number of décors in *Sentimental Education,* for just as the political reformers collect bits and pieces of laws and institutions that they like from every past source, the decorators of public and private spaces collect their favorite objects and motifs from different eras and throw them together. The Alhambra dance hall is perhaps the most flagrant example of this tendency, and its description emphasizes nothing if not variety:

Two parallel arcades in the Moorish style extended right and left. . . . the fourth side, where the restaurant lay, was designed to look like a Gothic cloister with stained-glass windows.

A sort of Chinese roof sheltered the platform on which the musicians played; the ground all around it was covered with asphalt, and there were some Venetian lanterns hung on poles which, seen from a distance, formed a crown of multicoloured lights above the dancers. Every few yards there stood a pedestal supporting a stone basin from which a slender jet of water rose into the air. In the shrubberies plaster statues could be seen, Hebes and Cupids . . . . (80)

Luxury seems to be defined here by a collection of exotic architectural and decorative clichés: Arab, medieval, Oriental, Italian, classical.

Although newly opened when Frédéric and his friends go there, the Alhambra has been designed with no style of its own or for its time. Its appeal must lie in the fact that is a collection of elements from elsewhere and from the past. Virtually every furnished and decorated interior space in *Sentimental Education* is likewise made up of heterogeneous, collected objects: the Arnoux boutique and house, the successive lodgings of Frédéric and Rosanette, the Dambreuse mansion. The phenomenon of collecting was still relatively recent in Flaubert's time, an invention of the nineteenth-century middle class that was often commented on as a new practice during the July Monarchy. Collecting implies a relation to style based on the acquisition of objects, as opposed to the commissioning of artists or artisans to produce new ones. If collecting is thus a "bourgeois" phenomenon in the economic sense of the term, it is also bourgeois in the pejorative sense used by artists concerned with their autonomy, for it shifts aesthetic decisionmaking from producers (designers or decorators) to the consumers (collectors). Moreover, by resurrecting and relegitimating styles from the past, collecting detracts from efforts by the present-day community of decorative producers to develop styles in accordance with recent practices and technical innovations, and to win acceptance for these new creations.

The indiscriminate mixing of styles is accompanied by a blurring of the distinction between high art and decorative crafts. The very existence of such a distinction, of course, is not universal, but is a socially and historically determined phenomenon, so that the loss of the distinction should not be regarded as a crime against the nature of art but simply as a shift in the social categories in which objects are placed. Nonetheless, several passages in *Sentimental Education* imply that art is a distinct category, and that the objects that belong to it should not be judged by the criteria of utility or economic worth, or compared to the nonart objects that can be thus judged. This assumption clearly underlies the treatment of Hussonnet's periodical, *Le Flambard,* which is described as "treating a book of poems and a pair of boots in exactly the same style" (235). (There is surely an allusion here to Théophile Gautier's remark, in his famous art-for-art's-sake manifesto of 1835, the preface to *Mademoiselle de Maupin,* that he "should be more willing to go without boots than without poems.")[25] Given this distinction between what is art and what is not, and the special status implicitly conferred on the former, references to the confusion of these categories can be read as not only descriptive, but prescriptive. *Sentimental Education* purports to tell us how art is treated by the mid-nineteenth-century bourgeoisie, and strongly suggests that this treatment is a symptom of pettiness and decadence.

Rosanette's boudoir provides a subtle instance of this implied critique of artistic decadence. She herself, a workers' daughter turned courtesan, is hardly a member of the bourgeoisie, but her lodgings are furnished by bourgeois protectors and/or calculated to please them, and Frédéric is duly impressed. The room's most striking feature is the varied nature of many of its objects: a Turkish divan, black furniture inlaid with brass, a dais covered with swan's skin, ostrich feathers, a Bohemian bowl. Romantic exoticism and rarity of materials seem to be the dominant principles. On the ceiling, however, is something quite different—much more French and much more traditionally artistic: "in a gilded wooden frame, cupids frolicked on pillowy clouds in an azure sky" (123–24). In one sense this painting fits in quite well: it is a merely decorative work, with no claim to artistic distinction, and it introduces yet another form of variety, that of time, because it strongly suggests an eighteenth-century style. But the style it suggests is that of Boucher, and this recalls the exchange between Arnoux and Pellerin in which the latter was reminded that he had promised to furnish two Boucher-style panels. Frédéric, who once admired Pellerin for his fiery art-for-art's-sake idealism, is now dazzled by the sort of hackwork that the painter was ashamed to admit to producing. He is impressed because the decor signifies wealth and the pleasures it can buy, pleasures he now desires far more than the artistic success he had once prized.

Frédéric's pursuit of the pleasures of wealth also determines him to frequent the Dambreuses, the quintessential representatives of the upper bourgeoisie. Their house is described several times, always with emphasis on the profusion of tasteful luxury items. The following example shows the way art fits into one of these descriptions:

> The great candelabra, like fiery bouquets, spread their light over the hangings and were reflected in the mirrors; and at the far end of the dining-room, the walls of which were lined with a jasmine-covered trellis, the buffet looked like the high altar of a cathedral or a jeweller's window-display, there were so many dishes, dishcovers, knives, forks, and spoons, in silver and silver-gilt, in the midst of cut-glass flashing its iridescent light across the food. The other three drawing-rooms were overflowing with works of art: landscapes by old masters on the walls, ivory and porcelain on the tables, and Chinese curios on the consoles: lacquer screens stood in front of the windows, bouquets of camellias filled the fireplaces; and the soft strains of music could be heard in the distance, like the hum of bees. (161–62)

The most notable feature of this passage is that its own artistry—the similes, the exquisite images of colored and reflected light—comes to an abrupt end when the subject changes from food to art. The description of the artworks contains no metaphoric language, no subordinate clauses; its form is that of enumeration and parataxis (successive parallel clauses without conjunction or subordination). This stylistic contrast suggests that at the Dambreuse reception, the real work of art and center of interest is the magnificent spread of food, and that the *objets d'art* merely fill space elegantly. The order in which they are listed, moreover, suggests a descent from the rare and unquestionably artistic to the commonplace and even natural: old master paintings, ivory and porcelain pieces, curios, screens, bouquets. The artworks and decorations interest no one in themselves; what matters is that they are all there, signifying opulence. So many fill the room that their artistic qualities go unnoticed. The passage ends with a commonplace simile, which repeats the themes of descent from art to nature and loss of differentiation: the faint music is "like the hum of bees."

A drawing room description during another of Frédéric's visits to the Dambreuses suggests an even more complete disregard for artworks: "In spite of the lamps standing in the corners, the light was dim; for the three windows were wide open, and formed three broad rectangles of darkness side by side. The spaces in between, under the pictures, were occupied by flower-stands five or six feet high; and a silver teapot with a samovar was reflected in a mirror in the distance. There was a discreet murmur of voices, and shoes could be heard squeaking on the carpet" (236). Here paintings are reduced to points of reference, whose existence informs us that there is space on the walls between the windows and above the flower stands. (It is interesting to note that the sequence of elements in this passage is strikingly similar to the one analyzed above: light, pictures, other decorative objects, sounds, noise.) The Dambreuses possess artworks, but neither they nor their guests notice them. The sense of indifference to true art and confusion of categories is reinforced a few sentences later when Frédéric compares Madame Dambreuse herself to a work of art: "she was leaning back a little, with the tip of her foot on a cushion, as calm as some delicate work of art or rare flower" (236–37).

This contemplation of Madame Dambreuse is not the first time, of course, that desire has led Frédéric to confuse art and sentiment. His vague wish to write or paint depended on just such a confusion, which was perpetuated by his preoccupation with the Arnoux couple. Because Madame Arnoux was surrounded by a universe of objects associated with her husband's trades, Frédéric's idealized love becomes inextricably bound up with the commercial prostitution of art. He begins by confusing her with the heroines of novels, and soon "her gloves, her rings were things of special significance to him, as important as works of art" (66). Arnoux's declining career entails the dissipation of the set of objects associated with his wife, and parallels the degradation of Frédéric's passion. Upon his return to Paris in part 2, "finding Madame Arnoux in a setting which was unfamiliar to him, he had the impression that she had somehow lost something, that she had suffered a vague degradation" (116). Bored and annoyed after Arnoux shows him his shop littered with pottery, Frédéric projects his disillusion onto the object of his love: "What an ordinary creature she is!" (117). He again degrades her image in his mind after his visit to Arnoux's second-rate pottery factory north of Paris, where she has not only refused his entreaties but also has been corrupted in his eyes by her association with the vulgarities of manufacturing and her defense of Sénécal's harshness to a worker: "She's a fool, a goose, a beast, let's forget about her" (203). As Arnoux's financial difficulties mount, he exploits the young man's love by sending his wife to ask him to intervene in his favor with Monsieur Dambreuse. By the time Arnoux has fallen to being a dealer in ecclesiastical objects, still prostituting the notion of art by calling his establishment "The Gothic Art Shop," Frédéric has betrayed his great love by sleeping regularly with two other women, and he flees the shop when Madame Arnoux appears (389).

Explaining to Frédéric why he has left dealing in art for manufacturing pottery, Arnoux says, "What can a fellow do in an age of decadence like ours? Great painting has gone out of fashion. Besides, you can introduce art into every sphere of life. You know how devoted I am to the cause of beauty!" (116). These words are surely self-serving, and they may be naïve in their assumption that cultural change implies decadence, but they contain more than a grain of truth. Art need not be a search for greatness and transcendence, and there is no reason to disdain the more modest goal of making attractive objects that can give pleasure in daily life. Flaubert may well have thought that he was satirizing Arnoux's ideas, but one of the merits of his novel is that it lets us hear many different voices and points of view, so that we can judge them ourselves in accordance with the interests of our time.

Arnoux says that his career change was inevitable, and nothing in the novel contradicts him. *Sentimental Education* proposes no solution to the predicaments of art that it portrays. Nowhere does Flaubert suggest that if Arnoux were less vulgar or Pellerin more disciplined their failure might have been avoided. No character's artistic views or practices transcend those of others to serve as an example of what might be. More important, no scheme is advanced for reforming the social or economic status of art, unless one wants to count the sinister political moralism of

Sénécal or Pellerin's ludicrous demands for government help. Even the criticism of "industrial art," described in this chapter, remains implicit. This absence of overt judgments and prescriptive ideals is characteristic of Flaubert's concept of the novelist's relation to his work: "An author in his book must be like God in the universe, present everywhere and visible nowhere" (*Letters,* 1:173).

Sentimental Education has, however, a singular moment in which an alternate relation to art for one character is presented and endorsed by the narrator:

> Frédéric did not go to see [Arnoux and his wife] again; and, to take his mind off his disastrous passion, he took up the first subject which occurred to him, and began to write a history of the Renaissance. He heaped his desk pell-mell with humanists, philosophers, and poets; he went to the Print Room to see engravings of Marcantonio; and he tried to understand Machiavelli. Gradually his work exerted a soothing influence on him. He forgot his own personality by immersing it in that of others—which is perhaps the only way to avoid suffering from it. (188)

Here, the narrator seems to say, is what might have saved Frédéric: hard work and the doctrine of impersonality. Admittedly, if we take Frédéric's behavior patterns seriously we must suppose that if Madame Arnoux—sent by her husband this time—had not come to interrupt this literary interlude, some other distraction would have soon brought Frédéric back to his usual ways. We may also doubt that he was capable of writing a worthwhile history of the Renaissance. But the possibility of a life devoted to losing oneself in others through literature is never denied. It is a strictly individual remedy, one which implies no solution to the social or economic problems of art, but it is a possible positive choice for Frédéric Moreau, the man of infinite negative choices. It is surely the choice of Flaubert, the positive action that made Flaubert's artistic refusal of all forms of social belonging something different from Frédéric's passive failure to belong.

Frédéric's brief success at obtaining calm through literary work is the closest the novel comes to defining its hero's relation to its author:

Frédéric is Flaubert as he might have been without the choice of becoming an artist through sheer determination and hard work. In his groundbreaking study of *Sentimental Education*, the sociologist Pierre Bourdieu writes: "Frédéric is indeed one of Gustave's possibles, never completely left behind: through him and everything he represents, we are reminded that aesthetic disinterestedness is rooted in practical disinterest and indetermination chosen as a style of life in indetermination suffered as a destiny. What if intellectual ambition were only the imaginary inversion of the failure of temporal ambitions?"[26] Bourdieu's analysis may strike us as a cruel deflation of the admiration we customarily pay to the artistic or intellectual life, yet his conclusion is perhaps simply a way of restating one of Flaubert's most memorable remarks on the power of literature. "The only way of tolerating existence," he wrote to Mademoiselle Leroyer de Chantepie in September 1858, "is to lose oneself in literature as in a perpetual orgy" (*Pléiade*, 2:832).

7

Narration and Free Indirect Discourse

The remark that one can avoid suffering from one's own personality only by immersing oneself in others through study is highly atypical of *Sentimental Education*, not because of the idea expressed but because the narrator expresses an explicit opinion at all. Flaubert's often-repeated doctrine of impersonality has a formal counterpart in the detachment of his narration, the virtual absence of a narrator with a distinct personality. *Sentimental Education* has no identifiable storyteller, and one of the challenges it poses to readers and critics is that of understanding what happens to the storyteller's function in this long and polished written narrative.

The different forms of printed fiction—novels, romances, novellas, short stories—are genres characteristic of the modern world, especially the world of private leisure that grew out of the transformation of the feudal nobility into a court nobility and, even more important, the increasing importance of the middle classes. The novel emerged as an important genre in the seventeenth century, and by the early nineteenth century it was arguably the most popular and influential literary form and was bidding to become the most prestigious as well. Reading printed fiction is a very different sort of activity from listening to a storyteller, and yet it draws on the forms and practices of oral (and manuscript) narrative, both transforming and replacing its predecessors. Some printed fiction evokes oral tradition explicitly by beginning with a storytelling situation; examples include Joseph Conrad's *Heart of Darkness* and many of Guy de Maupassant's short stories and tales. The nineteenth-century novel, however, generally does not rely on this kind of self-situating device, so that its dependence on the printed book and on individual, private reading is not disguised. The printed word is essentially portable; unlike the story told by someone real or fictional, the novel belongs to no place, no circle of relationships and conversations.

Readers of novels, however, often react *as if* someone were telling them a story, even while remaining aware that they are reading prose in a book. Many novelists encourage this response by writing in the voice of an identifiable narrator who engages in the sort of linguistic behavior storytellers use with their listeners: the narrator can try to charm, explain, flatter, educate, preach, and so forth. When speech acts such as these are imitated in print narration, they create an illusion of human contact and social relationship between teller and listener. This is quite a different use of language, both in form and intent, from simply dispensing information while assuming that someone is listening or reading. An important part of narration, what we might call *narrative* proper (as opposed to *discourse* occurring in narration), does indeed consist in the giving of information, and this function generally takes on linguistically specific forms, such as the use of the third person and the past tense, and the absence of any reference to the situation of the speaker and the listener. These features of narrative proper, however, are rarely sustained without interruption throughout a work.

Although Flaubert's major predecessors in the novel of society and manners usually wrote without named, explicitly characterized narrators, the narration in their works includes discursive elements that establish some personal relation to the reader. The narrator of Sand's *Indiana,* for example, is a man who confides his sympathetic but limited moral judgments to the reader. Stendhal includes asides to future readers, those of 1880 or 1930, thereby commenting on society, historical change, and his expectation of being misunderstood by his contemporaries. Balzac's narrator is a tireless pedagogue, psychological analyst, and political edi-torialist whose task is nothing less than that of explaining to the reader the workings of the modern world.

We need look no further than the opening sentences of *Memoirs of a Madman, November,* and the first *Sentimental Education* to verify that Flaubert's early fiction makes obvious use of the discursive devices by which printed narration imitates the personal contact of teller and listener:

> Why write these pages? What are they good for?—What do I know about it myself? It's pretty stupid, in my opinion, to go asking people the motive of their actions and their writings. Do you know yourself why you've opened these miserable pages that a madman's hand will write? (*Memoirs of a Madman*)

> I like autumn, this sad season goes well with memories. (*November*)

> The hero of this book, one October morning, arrived in Paris with a heart of eighteen years and a diploma in letters. (first *Sentimental Education*)

The first of these beginnings is aggressively personal and intrusive, sug-gesting a speaker tormented by stage fright who lashes out at the audi-ence. The second makes us feel that we are going to get to know the narrator as he reveals his tastes. The third places more emphasis on narra-tive proper, but begins by reminding us that we are starting to read a book, just as at the theater the dimming of lights and the raising of a cur-tain remind us that what we are about to see is a play.

In the first chapter of *Madame Bovary,* Flaubert explicitly rids his novel of this kind of personal, discursive narrator. The opening sentence seems to be spoken by an identifiable narrator who was a witness to the action he describes, an intermediary between us and the action: "We were in the study room, when the Principal entered, followed by a *new kid* dressed in street-clothes and by a monitor who was carrying a large desk." Soon, however, the *we* of the opening sentence becomes less and less frequent, and many things are told about the new pupil that an old classmate could hardly be expected to know. The text seems to pass quickly from narration by a characterizable witness to narration by an anonymous and impersonal figure speaking only in the third person. A few pages later, just as we are getting used to this transformation, we come upon a sentence that returns to the discursive mode of the personal narrator, but that does so only to deny the possibility that the story we are reading could be based on firsthand testimony, as we might at first have been led to believe: "It would now be impossible for any of us to remember anything about him." Henceforth the story will be told by an almost impersonal narrator, whose few discursive interventions do not add up to a sense of an individual voice.

The narration of *Sentimental Education* is impersonal from the outset. Flaubert's stylistic mastery consists not in convincingly imitating a narrator's presence, but in producing a supple prose, taut or fluid as the subject demands. Unlike the beginnings used by Flaubert from *Mémoires d'un fou* to *Madame Bovary,* the opening paragraphs of his late novels make no reference to a narrator, to a relation between teller and listener, or to the act of writing or reading. Rather than be intrigued or encouraged by a narrator, the reader must simply accept as a matter of convention that a story is being told and that it may be worthwhile to follow it. The reader's relation to the story is simply that of a consumer to the product that he or she has decided to consume; it is not directed or mediated by a simulated relation between a teller and a listener. The reader's interest must be maintained by the story itself (in other words, by the information being conveyed about a fictional world and actions) or by the pleasures of good prose, but not by the traditional seductions of storytellers.

What, however, can possibly be meant by "the story itself"? It is one thing to avoid explicit imitation of a human narrator, and quite another to suggest that a story could exist without any telling. Information is not simply conveyed about a fictional world: authors choose ways of conveying it and patterns of organizing it without which it would not be informative at all. As discussed in Chapter 4 herein, the manner and order in which events are presented and things described is every bit as much a part of the narrative message as are the events and things themselves.

Indeed, one must go further and say that, in fiction at least, no events or things exist apart from their narrative presentation.

If we tried to pare a story down to the narrative proper, in the strictest sense, we might get something such as: "People came hurrying up; a steamboat moved off; a man sighed"—a string of third-person clauses in the past tense with nothing to characterize their speaker or to convey that speaker's attitude toward either the events or the listener. Flaubert may sometimes write a sentence of this form, but his text never remains in such a purely narrative mode for very long. There are always discursive as well as strictly narrative elements: descriptions, conjunctions and other expressions of sequence or relation, words said or thought by characters. The absence of a personal narrator, in other words, implies neither objectivity nor pure narrativity. Between the fictional world and the reader stands not the mediating figure of a human narrator, but a different kind of mediation that includes the order of presentation of events, their relation to description and dialogue, and the language and style that give them existence and form.

The words of characters—whether in dialogue or monologue, spoken aloud or thought in silence—present specific problems in the mediation between fictional worlds and readers. Characters' words are events in the fictional universe, so that they are part of what narrative tells about, and yet as words to be read they can be part of the narrative in a way that things and nonverbal events cannot. In his discussion of poetry in Book III of *The Republic,* Plato distinguished between imitation (*mimesis*), in which a poet speaks in the voice of a character, and narrative (*diegesis*), in which a poet speaks in his own voice (and may speak *about* what characters say). He defined drama by its exclusive use of mimesis, lyric or dithyrambic poetry by its complete reliance on diegesis. Epic poetry is a mixture of the two, in which the poet both narrates in his own right and imitates the speeches of characters. The novel, like most narrative genres, resembles the epic in being both *mimetic* and *diegetic.* Flaubert mixes the two modes in presenting Frédéric's first conversation with Arnoux. We read in quotation marks Arnoux's words, "the force of each piston stroke, at so many a minute" (*mimesis*), but what the art dealer says next is reported in the phrase, "he expatiated on the beauties of the landscape" (*diegesis*).

Imitation (direct discourse of characters) places the listener or reader *as if* in the immediate presence of the character, whereas narrative (diegesis) implies the mediating presence of a narrator who decides how to summarize, describe, and relate what was said. Flaubert's major achievement in narration was to fuse these two forms into a narrative discourse characterized by a subtle interplay of perspective between the narrator and the characters. The narrator's mediating role often seems purely formal: a distance is maintained between the reader and the characters, yet no voice of commentary is identifiable. The most important ingredient of this impersonal yet fluid narration is a deceptively simple technique known as *free indirect discourse (style indirect libre)*.

Indirect discourse is a grammatical transformation of direct discourse. Instead of, "He said, 'I am so happy to have escaped from business,'" Flaubert writes, "He said how happy he was to have escaped from business" (17). This is ordinary indirect discourse, and it is the next sentence in the passage commented on above, which already included direct discourse and diegesis. It is not *free* indirect discourse because the indirect, third-person transformation is bound to its original speaker by an introductory phrase ("he said . . ." or "he said that . . ."). But Flaubert could have written the sentence, "He was happy to have escaped from business." The discourse is now both indirect (transformed into the third person) and free (unattributed).

We may wonder, however, whether the sentence, "He was happy to have escaped from business," should be interpreted as part of the character's discourse at all, or whether it is not purely diegetic, a report by the narrator on Arnoux's sentiments. This uncertainty is real, and it is both the peril and the promise of free indirect discourse. It makes point of view ambiguous and raises questions about how we know what we know: if we think Arnoux said it, how can we be sure? if we think it is the narrator's comment, how does the narrator know what Arnoux thought—is the narrator omniscient, or did he hear Arnoux say it, in which case it is not the narrator's comment anymore?

To pursue the implications of these questions, let us leave this hypothetical example made from a sentence in which Flaubert did not use free indirect discourse and turn to some in which he did. The first problem with free indirect discourse is identifying it. There are many cases in which the status of free indirect discourse is ambiguous and subject to disagreement, but there are also cases where its presence and function are evident. We shall begin with some of these in an attempt to identify clues to the presence of free indirect discourse and discuss the problems of its interpretation.

Sometimes free indirect discourse is signaled quite directly in a preceding phrase, as in this example from the first chapter:

> Little by little Frédéric calmed down, and he gave his attention to what his servant was saying.
>
> Monsieur's arrival was impatiently awaited. Mademoiselle Louise had cried to be allowed to go in the carriage to meet him. (23)

The first sentence strongly implies that what follows will be "what his servant was saying." To continue with, "The servant said that Monsieur's arrival . . ." would be redundant. The attribution is already clear and has no more ambiguity than indirect discourse. At most, the reader is required to take a slightly more active role in linking the two paragraphs than would be the case if the free form had not been used. Most readers, however, probably would feel that the situation is obvious and that they are not interpreting anything. The effect can be both clear and natural, as in this sentence referring to Madame Dambreuse: "Everybody praised her self-abnegation; she was behaving like a true mother" (135).

Sometimes the presence of free indirect discourse can be inferred not from what precedes it but from what follows, in that it becomes retrospectively clear that what was just communicated to the reader has also been communicated from one character to another. Here is the exchange that ensues when Monsieur Roque interrupts Frédéric and Deslauriers during their evening conversation in Nogent:

"So you're back in our parts?" he went on. "Excellent! I heard about it from my little girl. Keeping well, I hope? You're not leaving us again, are you?"

And off he went, doubtless put out by Frédéric's cool reception.

The truth of the matter was that Madame Moreau was not on calling terms with old Roque. He lived in illicit union with his housekeeper and was held in very low esteem, for all that he was the electoral registrar and Monsieur Dambreuse's steward.

"The banker who lives in the Rue d'Anjou?" Deslauriers asked.

(29)

Deslauriers's question can only be a response to the mention of Dambreuse, which must have been made by Frédéric. At this point we realize that the whole preceding paragraph ought to be taken as Frédéric's explanation of why he had not greeted Monsieur Roque more warmly. Perhaps its introductory phrase, "The truth of the matter was . . . ," should be read as slightly reticent or grudging response to an inquiry or remark from Deslauriers, who might even be presumed to have said something such as, "He was doubtless put out by your cool reception."

We can say that in this example the *communicative context* signals the presence of free indirect discourse, which is recognizable because of its necessary place in an exchange between characters. Communicative context enables us to identify free indirect discourse when it is used as part of a dialogue, as in this exchange between Frédéric and Madame Arnoux:

"I leave him free enough! He had no need to lie!"

"Certainly not," said Frédéric.

It was probably the result of his way of life, he had not thought about it, and perhaps in more important matters . . . .

"What do you mean by more important matters?"

"Oh, nothing."

Frédéric bowed his head, with an obedient smile. All the same, Arnoux possessed certain qualities: he loved his children.

"Oh, he does all he can to spoil them!"

> That was due to his easy-going nature; because after all, he was a good fellow. (171–72)

The unattributed sentences must be Frédéric's, because Madame Arnoux responds to them. The use of free indirect discourse creates no uncertainty here, but it makes our perception of the dialogue asymmetrical. Madame Arnoux's vehement protests are given directly, as are Frédéric's immediate expressions of agreement. His defenses of her husband, however, are all in the free indirect mode, placed as if at a distance from Frédéric. This distance underscores the strangeness of what he is doing: why should he be upsetting the woman he loves by defending her husband at the very moment when she has confided in him? The free indirect discourse suggests that his ill-timed words are an involuntary reaction to the criticisms of Arnoux rather than an appropriate response to Madame Arnoux's expressions of frustration. Frédéric has become so accustomed to defending Arnoux against Pellerin's and Sénécal's criticism that the words come almost automatically to his lips. The contrast between the direct and free indirect modes makes Frédéric seem at best a distracted, halfhearted participant in the dialogue, at worst a puppet of the phrases he has grown accustomed to repeating.

Despite Flaubert's deft use of it in dialogue, free indirect discourse in *Sentimental Education* cannot be understood, in most instances, solely on the basis of communicative context. Consider the short paragraph that follows the announcement to Frédéric and his mother that Louise Roque's mother has died: "All things considered, this death was not a calamity for anybody, not even for the child. The girl would only be the better for it later on" (107). This might seem like a narrator's judgment of the situation, but we know that Madame Moreau and her circle have a low opinion of Roque and his housekeeper, and we can also suppose that this kind of mean-spirited remark is much more appropriate to a respectable provincial widow than to a narrator who until this point has never descended to such pettiness. Madame Moreau might even be thinking of a possible marriage between her son and Louise, which would explain her glee at seeing a bad influence and source of social discredit removed from the girl's life. In other words, it is a *social context* that enables us to perceive the free indirect discourse. The situation is similar in the discussion of reactionaries after the 1848 revolution. The sentence, "And on top of this there was socialism too!" could, of course, be the comment of an indignantly conservative narrator, but we need not worry that the story is suddenly being recounted by a political partisan, for the remark fits perfectly into the reactionary milieu being described.

One may object that social context is far less clearly definable than communicative context. This is true, and it underscores an important point: the determination of what is free indirect discourse is not an exact science, nor is it meant to be. We may be able to describe and even classify certain kinds of contexts that strongly suggest the presence of the free indirect mode, but concepts such as social or communicative context will yield few certainties. Context is, by definition, an environment in the universe of discourse, and it often refers to a local environment— what is happening in a few sentences or paragraphs. Contexts are too local, too varied, too close to being unique for any satisfactory rules to be available for the interpretation of a phenonenon that depends on context. In the case of free indirect discourse, the reader must in effect ask each time: what makes more sense, for a narrator or a character to be making this statement? Very often, attentive readers of the novel will be able to answer this question to their satisfaction, but not always.

One way of looking at this approach to the free indirect mode involves the characterization of the narrator. When readers ask, "Is this a statement that the narrator would make?", they are assuming that they can get to know the narrator, like a fictional character or a real person, so as to judge what behavior to expect. Consider the sentences that follow Frédéric's chance encounter with the Arnoux shop: "Why had he not thought of her earlier? It was Deslauriers' fault" (32). The first sentence might belong to a narrator given to asking dramatic, rhetorical questions; the second, to a narrator who makes peremptory judgments. Neither one seems appropriate to the aloof and muted narration of Flaubert's novel. Obviously the examples described above as dependent on social context are related to the narrator as well, since the appropriateness of a statement to a character can be matched by the inappropriateness of the same statement to the narrator.

The problem with trying to characterize the narrator in Flaubert's novels is that the narrator is not anything like what we usually mean by a character. There are no personal attributes, no evident prejudices or opinions, no emotional attachments. In fact, if the narrator can be characterized at all, it is precisely by this absence of particulars. We find no narrator, if by a narrator we mean a figure with a personlike set of traits or habits. Trying to characterize the narrator is thus an exercise in futility, although we can develop a sense that some kinds of statements must be associated with the characters and not with the narrator.

Even the keenest reader of the novel, however, can never fully distinguish between, on the one hand, narrative, and on the other hand, imitation carried out in the free indirect mode. The most important consequence of this mode of narration is the blurring of the frontier between narrator and character, between narrative and imitation. This loss of separation is perhaps most evident in the use of free indirect discourse for the inner monologues or thoughts of characters, when no communicative or social situation is given to provide contextual clues as to whose statements are being reported. Consider this paragraph from the account of Frédéric's trip to Fontainebleau with Rosanette:

> He felt certain that he was going to be happy for the rest of his days, his contentment struck him as so natural, so inseparably linked with his life and this woman. He felt an urge to murmur endearments to her. She responded with affectionate words, little taps on the shoulder, and gentle caresses whose unexpectedness delighted him. Altogether he discovered an unsuspected beauty in her, a beauty which was perhaps only a reflection of their surroundings, unless their secret potentialities had brought it to the surface (325).

Distinguishing here what belongs to the narrator and what belongs to the character may indeed be possible. The first sentence describes Frédéric's feelings, but does so in a language probably too abstract and general to be used by someone talking or thinking about himself. The expansive rhythm and discreet parallelisms identify the sentence's lyricism more with the stylist than with the protagonist. The abrupt change in tone of the next sentence, which is brief, direct, and concrete, reminds us that the stylist is fully in control, and increases the distance between narrator and character because Frédéric's feelings are now being described reductively, almost mockingly. The third sentence, which describes Rosanette but also Frédéric's reaction to her, is less cutting, but, like the first sentence, it maintains its distance from him by producing a three-point summary of her actions that seems too neat and rhetorical for a lover to utter to himself.

The paragraph's last sentence raises the most doubts about the status and perspective of the narration. "Discovering an unsuspected beauty" in someone is something that lovers not only do but think about doing: this might be a phrase that Frédéric would say to himself. This possibility is borne out by the last two clauses, which offer mutually contradictory explanations of Rosanette's newfound beauty. We know by now that Frédéric is given to being swayed by whatever thought is passing through his head at a given moment. Here he seems to try out different possibilities as they occur to him, each idea generating the next in a virtual parody of the thesis/antithesis/synthesis paradigm of French scholastic rhetoric. (Thesis: she has unsuspected beauty. Antithesis: it is only a reflection of our surroundings. Synthesis: the secret potentialities of the surroundings have revealed her unsuspected beauty.) This kind of wheel-spinning thought process seems very much in accord with Frédéric's habitual indecision and empty cleverness, and attributing these phrases to him relieves us of feeling obliged to accept this contorted analysis of his sentiments toward Rosanette.

The problem with the analysis just attempted above is that it is both painstaking and subjective. No one reading the novel at a normal rate will stop to puzzle out this kind of fine distinction, and readers who linger over the passage will most likely disagree over which ideas and words are appropriate to Frédéric and which are not. Like most narrators, I have tried to buttress my version of things by making assertions I hoped the reader would share, or at least accept without making trouble. But will everyone agree that discovering unsuspected beauty is something lovers do and think about? Probably not. Would I agree myself if I were not writing a book on *Sentimental Education*? Not necessarily. To make the passage seem fully analyzable, I have had to add to it judgments and motivating statements of a kind that Flaubert's novel uses only sparingly.

Readers of Flaubert inevitably experience an indefinable blending of perspectives in passages such as the one analyzed here, and trying to sort everything out as explicitly as I have attempted to do here is pedantic and ultimately pointless. This type of analysis, however, is not without its uses. For one thing, its possibility shows that the text is not incoherent; readers who want to slow down and analyze it in great detail will not find themselves defeated by inconsistencies and contradictions. More important, the way in which we are forced to add assumptions to the text in order to make everything precise shows that Flaubert's narration allows for and even calls for an active reader. Even without making the assumptions of our reading explicit in a formal analysis, our minds must be adapting to the subtle shifts in perspective and language from one sentence to another. As readers, we must develop a feel for the slippage of discourse back and forth between the characters and the impersonal narrator, and yet we must accept that we will not be able to pin everything down. Readers must come to understand that the loss of clear boundaries between characters, or between characters and narrator, is not a defect but a revealing feature of Flaubert's fictional world.

Because characters are not unambiguously attached to their words and thoughts, it becomes impossible to determine to what extent these words and thoughts are really theirs. At one of the Dambreuse receptions, free indirect discourse is used to recount items of gossip that Frédéric hears: "Old Madame de Sommery had a cold; Mademoiselle de Turvisot was getting married; the Montcharrons were not coming back until the end of January; nor were the Bretancourts; people stayed longer in the country nowadays" (135). No attempt is made to attribute any of the remarks to anyone. The last three clauses suggest a conversation because each remark gives rise to the next, but that is as much coherence as can be found. The effect is not only to place the reader in the position of Frédéric overhearing strangers' gossip, but also to show that in some situations what is said has almost nothing to do with the individuals saying it and reveals almost nothing about them.

The reactionary chitchat at the Dambreuses, the speeches at the banker's funeral, the political griping that goes on when Frédéric's circle of acquaintances meets—all these are instances of utterances that seem to float free and disconnected from any individual consciousness or will. Free indirect discourse makes the narration into a patchwork of semi-attributed quotations, and the characters are often quoting things they have heard or simply filling a social role. Madame Dambreuse, for example, has a worldly grace devoid of personality. She simply follows polite and refined usage at every moment: "If somebody spoke of a sick person, she frowned anxiously, while she assumed a joyful expression if there was mention of balls or parties . . . if she made a commonplace remark, she put it in such a banal form that it was impossible to tell whether she had her tongue in her cheek or not" (135, 357). In this last respect Madame Dambreuse is like the narration itself, which always maintains an indefinable distance from the common or vulgar remarks and ideas it manages to incorporate.

The free-floating character of free indirect discourse taints every statement made in it with the suspicion of quotation and cliché. Speech reported in this mode seems less an utterance invented and controlled by its speaker than an available statement that fits the context and thus is made by someone, identifiable or not. When Madame Arnoux reproaches Frédéric for professing love for her while keeping Rosanette as his mistress, his response is robbed of vehemence or poignancy by being shunted into the free indirect mode:

> "Yes, you're right!" exclaimed Frédéric. "I don't deny it! I'm a brute! Listen to me!"
> If he had made her his mistress, it had been out of despair, like somebody committing suicide. What is more, he had made her very unhappy, to avenge his own shame on her.
> "What torments I have suffered! Don't you understand?" (353)

Communicative context ("Listen to me!") makes the status of the middle paragraph quite clear. The shift in mode of discourse, by emphasizing that the narrator is not responsible for the statements while removing the statements from Frédéric's direct utterance, leaves them in a kind of limbo, where as readers we can quickly become suspicious, for they sound like clichés out of melodramatic novels. Does Frédéric really believe this, we wonder, or are these simply the stock phrases that seem most expedient for the purpose of appeasing Madame Arnoux? If he does believe what he is saying, is that the limit of his self-understanding? Neither question is answerable, and that points to something absolutely crucial about narration and character in *Sentimental Education:* we have no access to any character's essence. There is no guarantee, and in fact no evidence, that characters *have* an essence, a stable inner being, or even psychological depth.

We know Frédéric essentially through the language of his utterances and feelings, to a lesser extent through his actions. The traditional assumption about character would be that these words, thoughts, and actions should be understood as the manifestations of a psychologically consistent self in control of its intentions and actions. When Balzac presents an ambitious young man, such as Rastignac in *Old Goriot,* everything about him can be understood in terms of that essence: ambitious young man. In *Sentimental Education,* however, the narration makes no claim to present a character's psychological essence, and the representation of thoughts and words is so distanced as to call into question the conventional—and naïve—inference that words correspond either to true feelings or to deliberate dissimulation. The characters, in the end, only exist at the level of their actions and utterances, so that any attempt to judge these as either sincere or false is likely to be inconclusive.

Not only do the characters exist *for the reader* only at the level of what they do and say (rather than what they *are*), but we have every reason to suspect that their existence *in and for themselves* (to adopt for a moment the fictional belief that they are real beings) is no deeper or more authentic. In the final conversation between Frédéric and Madame Arnoux, the exchange in which she fully acknowledges their love is followed by this two-sentence paragraph: "He regretted nothing. His former sufferings were redeemed" (414). In the French, the first sentence is in the *passé simple,* the definite past of narrative, whereas the second is in the imperfect, the tense of both description and free indirect discourse. The first statement, then, would seem to come from the impersonal narrator, whereas the second might be either a report on Frédéric's feelings or a transformation of what he says to Madame Arnoux. Deciding which is the case is impossible, and that undecidability strongly suggests that there is no difference between what Frédéric says and what he feels—if he says that his sufferings are redeemed, then for him at that moment they are, although nothing guarantees that this feeling of redemption is any more genuine or more durable than any other of Frédéric's feelings. In other words, Frédéric's personality is made up of the repertoire of actions and words he picks up from his culture and adopts, or applies to himself. His claim to possess a "beautiful soul"—or any other essence—is constantly belied by the mode of narration, which repeatedly shows him to be undistinguishable from the influences he has undergone, the language and mannerisms he has adopted.

The fluctuations of characters and the uncertainties of free indirect discourse are not the only features of the narration that make the reader of *Sentimental Education* take an active role in putting the story together. Many gaps and unspoken shifts in perspective occur between events as well. The reader must figure out that Arnoux is with one of his mistresses when Frédéric stops to visit and breaks a lady's parasol. The reader must also realize that the paper in which Arnoux wraps a bouquet for his wife before their departure from Saint-Cloud must be the note he received from from Mademoiselle Vatnaz, and that Madame Arnoux becomes upset over the bouquet because the note probably concerns her husband's relations with Rosanette. Perhaps some readers can even figure out just what goes on among Rosanette, Mademoiselle Vatnaz, and Delmar, beyond the obvious love triangle complicated by money. Occasionally a reader may go so far as to follow the financial and judicial mess that leads to Arnoux's bankruptcy and Frédéric's breakup with Rosanette. The text presents a wealth of unexplained or unconnected objects and events. In some cases the connections are fairly obvious; in others, not at all. What matters is that, easy or difficult, readers must to some degree serve as their own storytellers, filling in the explanatory and motivational gaps as they proceed, rather than relying on a narrator who tells them what they are supposed to know.

The reader cannot expect to sit back and be entertained by the story of *Sentimental Education*. Flaubert scorned the popular novelists who encouraged their readers to be nothing more than passive consumers of engrossing stories. "Where does the prodigious success of Dumas's novels come from?", he wrote Louise Colet in June 1853. "It's because you need no training to read them; their action is entertaining. So you're amused while you're reading them. Then, when the book is closed, since you're left with no impression and it has all flowed past like a clear stream, *you go back to your business*" (*Pléiade*, 2:358). In Flaubert's novels, readers must, in effect, train themselves, if only implicitly, to stitch together the often disconnected events, to sort out the shifts in voice and perspective. What is needed are not only reading skills but social skills: knowledge of the conventions of behavior and, above all, the habit of careful attentiveness to social surroundings and readiness to adapt accordingly.

The reader must be able to fit into the novel like a guest at a series of social events, from the elegant (Dambreuse receptions) to the humble (Dussardier's punch party). To understand quickly and unobtrusively how to act (and above all how to interpret the actions and words of others) in unfamiliar social situations is a skill traditionally emphasized in upper social strata; it is usually considered a mark of refinement or distinction. Readers of *Sentimental Education* need something of this savoir faire to construct a coherent and interesting story from the impersonal narration and shifting free indirect discourse of the novel. In other words, *Sentimental Education* is quite tangibly an elitist work in its very form, one designed to go against the reading practices of the masses in an age when literature was becoming a consumer product. Because the plot is not immediately engaging or amusing, the reader must not only cope with the subtlety of the style but also forego the most usual and immediate pleasures of stories in order to experience a more complex fictional universe.

Although the reader of *Sentimental Education* needs something of the savoir faire of a Madame Dambreuse, as opposed to the naïveté of a Dussardier or the rigidity of a Sénécal, the real elite for which Flaubert was writing was not the upper bourgeoisie but those who care about literature. He was crushed by the fact that his friend Louis Bouilhet died without reading the novel's last two chapters, and saddened that the critic Sainte-Beuve, who was one of the readers he had most in mind while writing it, died before it was published. By the time he finished *Sentimental Education,* Flaubert had come to like having his books sell and making some money from them, but what mattered the most to him was the reaction of the small band of writers whom he considered truly devoted to art. All others were bourgeois, whatever their socioeconomic standing. "Axiom: hatred of the Bourgeois is the beginning of virtue," he wrote to Sand in May 1867. "As for me, I include in the word bourgeois the bourgeois in overalls as well as the bourgeois in frock coat. It's we, we alone—that is, the educated—who are the People, or, to put it better, the tradition of Humanity" (*Letters,* 2:105). What Flaubert leaves unsaid here is that the kind of elite literary education and sensibility he is thinking of is much more fostered by society among the frock coats than among the overalls. Dussardier, the simple and goodhearted employee, is surely the most likeable character in the novel, but *Sentimental Education* would be completely out of place among the popular novels and tracts on his bookshelf.

Sentimental Education is a difficult book because its narration leaves some of the work of the storyteller to the reader. Like a storyteller, the novel narrates, imitates, describes, and presents events in order, but unlike a storyteller, it offers very few explanations, rarely invokes shared beliefs or attempts to impart knowledge, and makes no direct appeals to the reader's attention. The pieces of the narrative puzzle are presented in order, but the reader must still put them together, filling in gaps and interpreting ambiguities. In difficulty and uncertainty, reading *Sentimental Education* falls somewhere between listening to a carefully told story and trying to make sense out of events as they occur in real life. The novel's material is far more ordered and focused than are events in life, and yet it is not entirely packaged by someone for our amusement or instruction. Its reader must assume part of the storyteller's task of making sense of the stuff of life.

8

Dreams

In a rough outline of chapters probably dating from very early in his work on *L'Education sentimentale,* Flaubert gave titles to the three parts of his novel: "I. *Les Rêves* (*Dreams*) II. *La lutte* (*Struggle*) III. *l'Expérience* (*Experience*)."[27] In the end, he maintained his usual practice of using no titles for parts or chapters, and was probably wise to do so, for the provisional titles suggested a neater, more linear pattern of development than the actual novel was to provide. There are dreams and experience in every part of the novel; whether a struggle occurs anywhere in it is a question on which readers will probably disagree. Nonetheless, the titles do fit to a considerable degree: part 1 presents the hopes and ambitions of a young man and his friends, none of whom yet have the means of taking much action to realize their goals; part 2 follows the hero's slow immersion in the Parisian world, with its contrasting milieus and competing interests; part 3 chronicles the disillusionment accompanying both the long-awaited love affairs and the much-desired political revolution. Herein, I have chosen to adopt these titles for three chapters that, together with those devoted to beginnings and endings, form a commentary on the novel as it unfolds.

The first two chapters of *Sentimental Education* form a prologue or preamble to Frédéric's arrival and installation in Paris. Chapter 3 of part 1 begins with his visit to Monsieur Dambreuse, the banker whose acquaintance Deslauriers had urged Frédéric to cultivate. Dambreuse has followed a social trajectory that is the exact opposite of Frédéric's possible acquisition of his mother's noble title: the banker gave up his title, making his name sound bourgeois so that he might better fit into the world of finance. Frédéric's visit is brief and Dambreuse's welcome perfunctory. The descriptions create a contrast between, on the one hand, the drab compactness of Monsieur Dambreuse and his office, and, on the other hand, the expansive opulence surrounding Madame Dambreuse, whose "clothes seemed to fill the whole carriage" (32). The upper bourgeoisie is shown as having a double relationship to its wealth—grim and private acquisition, sumptuous and public consumption. This duality is identified with gender and age difference, since Monsieur Dambreuse does his harsh, inelegant dealing to possess, like an object, his young and attractive wife, and to allow her, in turn, to use and display the material objects that his money can buy.

Frédéric's long-planned call on Monsieur Dambreuse is followed, in a contrastive parallel typical of the structure of *Sentimental Education,* by his accidental first visit to *L'Art Industriel.* Here we find no contrast between the acquisition and consumption of wealth because the shop has the air of a domestic interior; Frédéric, indeed, will for some time nurture the idea that Madame Arnoux lives in an apartment above her husband's place of business. The Boulevard Montmartre shop seems capable of fusing contrasting aspects of bourgeois life—commerce and domesticity, earning and spending. Frédéric associates the shop with his dreams of transcending ordinary existence through art and romantic passion. Unlike the Dambreuse mansion, Arnoux's shop is open to the public, a contrast underscored by the juxtaposition of Frédéric's inability to get a response from the banker and his return visits to the art dealer's. An ambitious young man in the mold of Balzac's heroes would immediately set his sights on winning entry to the restricted, private world of the Dambreuses, but Frédéric's actions follow the path of least resistance, as we have seen, and he prefers to frequent *L'Art Industriel,* where he needs no invitation and where he can play the role of consumer rather than the more difficult part of social climber.

This proclivity to remain in the role of a spectator and occasional consumer defines Frédéric's relation to Paris throughout part 1 of the novel. For him Paris is a space defined by anonymity, multiplicity, confusion, an absence of belonging. He turns frequently to places of public yet solitary amusement: cafés, lectures, plays, reading rooms, shops, and boulevards. Walking on the Champs-Elysées amid the carriages of rich women, with whom he identifies not only Madame Dambreuse but also Madame Arnoux, "he felt as if he were lost in a remote world" (35). The metropolis is a spectacle of consumption, a stage for anonymous and objectified desire. In contrast to these glimpses of wealth and status, Frédéric's own lodgings are sordid, as is the restaurant where he can afford to dine. His attitude toward the people he encounters thus consists of either envy or disdain; in the case of his acquaintances Martinon and Cisy, it is a mixture of both. He envies Martinon's contentment and Cisy's refined manner, but disdains the former's conventionality and the latter's inferior mind. The combination of envy and disdain corresponds to Frédéric's social position as a not-yet-established member of a privileged class, and to his ambivalence toward bourgeois society. He is envious because he wishes to enjoy society and disdainful because he desires to transcend it. This ambivalence follows class and geographic lines: he wants to belong to the upper strata of Parisian society and to transcend those features of society most identified with modest circumstances and provincial life.

At the end of chapter 3, Frédéric is abandoning the dreams he shared with Deslauriers, giving up on the Dambreuse connection, and gradually forgetting his passion for Madame Arnoux. He seems well on the way to being merely a mediocre and rather solitary law student, enduring boredom and loneliness while he prepares for what is most likely to be a modest provincial career and an arranged marriage. His story is set in motion again at the beginning of chapter 4 by a political demonstration in December 1841, where he meets Dussardier and Hussonnet; the latter then reintroduces him to Arnoux. The demonstration itself leads to nothing of significance, and the reader's knowledge of it is virtually limited to Hussonnet's sardonic comments, but the use of a political protest to bring Frédéric back to his love and to his fascination with the art world is crucial to the structure of the novel. The students are protesting various aspects of the July Monarchy—its pro-English foreign policy, its conservative minister Guizot, and its resistance to electoral reform (that is, to the expansion of the right to vote, which was then restricted to a small group of wealthy men). In other words, the demonstration is an early manifestation of the republican and reform movements that would lead to the fall of the July Monarchy in February 1848. Its role in leading Frédéric back to Arnoux and his wife inaugurates the parallel between personal and political developments that will be pursued throughout the novel.

The demonstration's crucial but accidental role in Frédéric's life also illustrates the interplay between contingency and determinism in the novel. Without encountering Hussonnet, Frédéric might never have gone back to *L'Art Industriel,* and so this chance meeting underscores the *contingency* of the rest of the story, that other things might well have happened instead, and that the causal ordering we often find in events can only exist retrospectively, as an account of what actually happened and not as an explanation of what had to happen. Contingency is a major problem in historical explanation: when major events have causes so small that they seem to be mere accidents on the scale of history, then deterministic, predictive accounts have to be set aside—but can we accept "it was an accident" or "well, it just happened to go this way" as explanations at all? In his acclaimed one-volume history of the U.S. Civil War, James McPherson reviews the inadequacy of traditional, large-scale explanations of Union victory (greater population and industrial capacity, less internal division, better leadership late in the war, and so forth) by noting that on several occasions, the outcome of the conflict probably hung in the balance of small-scale tactical events on the battlefield, and that if these had gone differently historians would have been busy producing large-scale explanations of Confederate success. For McPherson, "the phenomenon of contingency can best be presented in a narrative format,"[28] and one can argue that few works of fictional narrative go as far as *Sentimental Education* in showing how contingency can be at work in chains of events that are structured and retrospectively coherent.

Nonetheless, the importance of the demonstration also suggests that Frédéric's life is caught up in forces of history over which he has no control. The student protests, we are told, are frequent; encountering one is simply an inevitable part of being a Parisian student in the early 1840s. Frédéric is apolitical, except for an occasional outburst of anti-authoritarian sentiment, but incidents such as these show that his private life is being swept along by the public events of his day and shaped by experiences that are not uniquely personal but rather shared with other members of his generation. There is no contradiction between this kind of determinism and the element of contingency discussed above, for whereas large-scale social events have the force of inevitability for the individual who interacts with them, the form and circumstances of that interaction can be a matter of accident. Frédéric could hardly have avoided the demonstration, whose occurrence is a given, but the way in which it leads him to Hussonnet, Dussardier, and then Arnoux can still be presented as a series of contingent events determined by nothing in particular.

Chapter 4 is dominated by Frédéric's entry into the *L'Art Industriel* circle, where he hopes to emulate artists and attract the attention of Madame Arnoux. It is also the chapter in which Frédéric's social circle, which already included Martinon and Cisy, takes shape: after Hussonnet and Dussardier, he meets Pellerin and Regimbart at Arnoux's, and the arrival of Deslauriers, who insists on including Sénécal, completes the group. Except for Pellerin and Regimbart, all are young men, and so Flaubert's claim to have written the moral or sentimental history of his generation largely rests on their portrayal. (Arnoux remains on the margins of this circle: he is older, and he does not attend the gatherings at Frédéric's or later at Dussardier's, although he mixes with many of the same individuals at the Alhambra and at Rosanette's masked ball.) The social situations of Pellerin and Regimbart give them something of the freedom and indeterminacy of youth, for the painter is at 50 unmarried and still in search of his first artistic success, and the "Citizen," though married, seems to have no fixed occupation and spends most of his time in cafés.

The young men who gather at Frédéric's on Saturdays come from different backgrounds and have different interests and ambitions, but all (except Dussardier) have in common a desire to become something more than what they currently are, and all (except Martinon) are united by their dislike (or even hatred) of Louis-Philippe's July Monarchy. Although only Hussonnet affects the style and mannerisms of artistic bohemia as popularized by Murger, the group as a whole is bohemian in a larger sense because of its youth, its desire, and its disdain for the bourgeois regime. In his 1840 story, "A Prince of Bohemia," Balzac had described bohemia as the Parisian country of talented young men trying to enjoy life while impatiently awaiting their chance to succeed in the larger society. He linked the bohemians' resentment of the established order to the phenomenon of *gerontocracy,* government by the old, a word coined under the Bourbon Restoration but to a large extent applicable to the July Monarchy as well.

The social historian Jerrold Seigel has advanced a definition of bohemia particularly useful in understanding the young men of *Sentimental Education.* "Bohemia grew up where the borders of bourgeois existence were murky and uncertain," he writes; "it was the appropriation of marginal life-styles by young and not so young bourgeois, for the dramatization of ambivalence toward their own social identities and destinies" (Seigel, 11). Hussonnet's eccentricity is merely the most obvious and dramatic form of marginality embraced in this group; other activities on the margins of the bourgeois life-style include Frédéric's desultory artistic activities, Sénécal's socialist fervor, Cisy's dandyism, and Deslauriers's and Martinon's love affairs with *grisettes.* The *grisettes* were young women of modest origins who worked in the Paris garment industry and lived independently, free from the tight behavior restrictions placed on unmarried women of the middle class. In bohemian mythology, and sometimes in real life, the *grisettes* became the mistresses of the students and struggling artists. Frédéric's disdain for both Deslauriers's and Martinon's relationships reflects both his idealistic passion for Madame Arnoux and his sense of social and aesthetic distinction: *grisettes* are too commonplace, and the easy joys of student love affairs with them too well-worn a cliché.

The bohemian ambivalence of Frédéric's circle toward conventional bourgeois life is nowhere more sharply expressed than in a conversation about women at one of the Saturday gatherings. Pellerin shows artistic eccentricity by preferring the beauty of tigers to that of women; Frédéric, thinking of Madame Arnoux, pleads in favor of "long black hair and big dark eyes," but Hussonnet reminds him that this is by now a commonplace, and poses as a libertine by implying that the only women who interest him are those of easy virtue. Then he tries to get the simple and modest Dussardier to agree with him: "Dussardier did not answer. They all urged him to tell what he preferred. 'Well,' he said, blushing, 'I'd like to love the same woman all the time!' He said this in such a way that there was a moment's silence; some of them were taken aback by this innocent declaration, while others perhaps recognized in it the unspoken desire of their own hearts" (68). Dussardier's remark astonishes because of its naïveté; it is precisely the sort of thing that a young man trying to impress others with his carefree, antiestablishment worldliness should never say. At the same time, Dussardier expresses the underlying desire of some of the young men not to renounce or challenge the bourgeois social order but to belong to it through a happy marriage. An insouciant or libertine disdain for marriage and fidelity is part of their social pose of opposition, most overtly expressed by the bohemian Hussonnet, and Dussardier's remark is an embarrassment because it forces them to recognize their ambivalence.

Frédéric's lack of a mistress is presented as a social liability rather than a sexual frustration. His passion for Madame Arnoux places him not only outside the paths of bourgeois ambition (represented by an affair with Madame Dambreuse and/or marriage to Louise Roque) but also outside the casual and sensual loves of students and *grisettes*. At the Alhambra ball, both Deslauriers and Arnoux reproach Frédéric for not leaving with a woman; when he objects that they have not done so either, Arnoux reminds him that he already has one—his wife—and Deslauriers promptly picks up the first attractive woman he encounters. What pains Frédéric is not chastity, but envy and humiliation. He manages to recover somewhat in his friend's eyes the next day after accompanying Cisy on an errand that is not explicitly described but that is presumably a trip to a brothel where both men lose their virginity. Frédéric tells Deslauriers about their expedition, suppressing the fact that he was as inexperienced as Cisy, and wins his friend's approval (87).

Women are not, however, the most frequent or important topic of conversation in Frédéric's circle; what occupies them most is politics. All except Martinon, the ultraconformist, despise the July Monarchy with a hatred that is intense, spontaneous, and unthinking. If they get along so well with one another, it is first of all because "their hatred for the government had all the loftiness of an indisputable dogma." Theirs is no rational critique of the regime, simply a distaste and resentment that go hand in hand with being young outsiders. Martinon's defense of Louis-Philippe is a social gaffe even worse than Dussardier's wish for lifelong love. When Martinon tries to speak up, "the others overwhelmed him with the commonplaces to be found in every newspaper" (67). This is a good example of the absence, in *Sentimental Education,* of a voice of truth or authority. Martinon is a ridiculously stodgy young man, certainly not a credible defender of the government in readers' eyes, but the others' arguments are no better, being merely journalistic clichés. Neither the regime's defender nor its opponents have any claim to being right, or to speaking for the author. Martinon defends the regime because he expects to find comfort and privilege under it, and the others—especially Deslauriers and Sénécal—denounce it out of resentment.

The reference to journalistic commonplaces is the first indication that the political culture and beliefs of the characters in *Sentimental Education* are largely derived from the press. The young men have little direct contact with political or governmental milieus, at least not until later in the book when some of them become regulars at the Dambreuse household. Their views are based neither on rational self-interest nor on thoughtful consideration of what is best for society, but rather on sentiment and media images. The lithograph of Louis-Philippe and his family all engaged in edifying occupations is "a source of delight to the middle classes, but the despair of the patriots" (62). Among the commonplace griefs against the July Monarchy thrown at Martinon are "Pritchard" and

"'Lord' Guizot," references to a largely symbolic affair over which the government's pro-English foreign policy was stigmatized as craven and unpatriotic. The political culture of *Sentimental Education* is that of a society in which the emotions of class conflict and individual situation become political positions by borrowing images and phrases from the commercial mass media.

The destinies of the young men of *Sentimental Education* are followed intermittently throughout parts 2 and 3, but the last chapters of part 1 are primarily devoted to Frédéric. Chapter 5, which contains the description of the Saturday gatherings and the account of the evening at the Alhambra, covers a year and a half of Frédéric's life, although "coverage" is hardly the appropriate concept for its loosely connected series of episodes. It is the first chapter in which the hero's passivity and indecision not only are important themes but also exert a clear influence on the narrative structure, so that the reader is forced to experience firsthand the lack of direction or consistency in Frédéric's life. The longest chapter by far of part 1, it has the least unity and provides a foretaste of the meandering, intermittent structure of part 2.

Near the beginning and near the end of the chapter are two parallel series of events: Frédéric takes a law exam, Hussonnet informs him that Arnoux has left Paris or that Madame Arnoux has returned, he delays his departure for Nogent so as to see her, learns that she is in fact not in Paris, and so has some extra time in Paris with nothing to do. The attendant circumstances change considerably, and the parallel is not so obvious as to make the chapter seem symmetrical or highly structured, but the reader experiences a confusing sense of déjà vu. Frédéric's life seems to be going in circles, even though the second time he passes, rather than fails, his examination, and is happy rather than melancholic during his stay in the half deserted Paris of summer. What unites the two series of events and makes them most difficult to distinguish for the reader is that both depend on Frédéric's obsession with grasping at circumstances that might create an opportunity for him to be alone with Madame Arnoux. He never attempts to create such opportunities, and so he overreacts whenever chance seems about to create one. His passivity thus leads directly to the insignificant twists and repetitions of the plot because he is

Dreams

constantly rearranging his life in response to events rather than trying to arrange events in his life.

Even on the two occasions in chapter 5 when Frédéric manages to be alone with Madame Arnoux, he is taking advantage of situations he did little to create, and he comes no closer to declaring his love. During his blissful walk through the streets with Madame Arnoux by his side, he decides to declare his love because "the opportunity was a good one" (77). As is often the case, he imitates a famous and energetic fictional character, but with no success. Here his model is Julien Sorel of Stendhal's *The Red and the Black,* who resolved to take Madame de Rênal's hand by ten o'clock or else kill himself. Walking with Madame Arnoux, Frédéric "gave himself as far as the Rue de Richelieu to declare his love," but they reach her destination before his self-imposed deadline, so that unlike Julien, he neither surmounts a crisis of will nor reveals his affection. Even his carriage ride with Madame Arnoux from Saint-Cloud to Paris, when he feels himself to be closer than ever to her, is the result of circumstances that Frédéric neither controls nor understands. Madame Arnoux is upset because of the bouquet her husband has given her, wrapped inadvertently in a note from Mademoiselle Vatnaz implying that Arnoux is hurrying back to Paris not for business, as he said, but to see his mistress. Seeing her crying, Frédéric feels that her sorrow creates a bond of complicity between them, but he fails to realize what has happened, and the bond of complicity exists only in his mind. Her daughter happens to be lying asleep between them in the carriage, and in kissing the little girl on the forehead, he feels himself to be showing affection to the mother, but Madame Arnoux merely tells him that he is kind because he is fond of children. His moments with her at Saint-Cloud and on this return journey will inspire him to succeed in his studies that year and will provide him with some of his fondest memories of her, but they are ordinary and fortuitous events given meaning and beauty only in his imagination and memory.

At the end of chapter 5, Frédéric, in Nogent for the late-summer vacation, learns from his mother that his inheritance will amount only to a modest income. Chapter 6 opens, in free indirect discourse, with his bitter and panic reaction: "Ruined, robbed, done for!" (99). This disaster

93

will be remedied nearly two and a half years later by his unexpected inheritance of his uncle's fortune, which brings him more than a tenfold increase in income. The long interlude in Nogent further illustrates the passivity of Frédéric, who lets himself be lulled by his mother's pleading and the comforts of home into all but giving up the Paris of his dreams. The temporary loss of wealth also affords an opportunity to explore two alternate destinies for Frédéric: the impoverished genius and the provincial. The first alternative to wealth he can think of is the bohemian myth of the great man struggling to avoid misery while creating masterpieces. "Perhaps poverty would increase his talents a hundredfold. He grew excited at the thought of all the great men who had worked in garrets. A soul such as Madame Arnoux's would surely be stirred by a sight of that sort" (100). As he so often does, Frédéric here sees his own life through the mediation of literary and journalistic clichés, and when his mother manages to postpone his return to Paris, the dream of becoming an impoverished genius simply fades away, replaced by other images and possibilities.

What first leads Frédéric to stay in Nogent, however, is not an image but the material comfort of provincial bourgeois life: "the comfort of his home corrupted him; he enjoyed having a softer bed, and napkins which were not torn" (100). Paris remains for him the place of his dreams and regrets, whereas Nogent is the site of an uninspiring but not unpleasant reality, a familiar routine that includes Sunday Mass and evening card games with his mother. Frédéric's relation to literature ceases to be that of even a would-be creator and becomes entirely that of a sentimental consumer, who sublimates his emotions by identifying them with what he reads. His readings and his letters to Deslauriers serve to dissipate both his dreams of life in Paris and his great passion for Madame Arnoux: "By dint of pouring his sorrow out in his letters, mingling it with his reading, taking it on his walks in the country, and spreading it everywhere, he had practically exhausted it" (105). He also tries to compensate for the loss of his literary ambitions by reading works of the romantics and of Shakespeare to Louise Roque, who is 12 when he returns to Nogent and who plays at being his wife. Monsieur Roque's interest in Frédéric and his desire to see Frédéric obtain the use of his mother's noble name suggest that he sees in him a future husband for his daughter, so that in educating Louise to his tastes, Frédéric may be trying to prepare for himself a provincial existence enlivened by a woman who can at least understand the dreams he will have given up.

Because of the vagueness of chronological references in *Sentimental Education,* the reader has no way of knowing that Frédéric has spent more than two years in Nogent until the letter arrives from Le Havre on 12 December 1845 announcing his inheritance. In fact, most readers probably will not have been aware that his return to Nogent came in August 1843, although that date can be deduced without too much difficulty from the progression of seasons and vacations since the story's beginning on 15 September 1840. It would seem that the novel can get by without any exact chronology at all, except for the precision of a few dates, such as that of the letter's arrival. What is structurally noteworthy is that in each of the novel's three parts, chronology remains a blur until punctuated by a precisely dated event near the end. In part 2, it is the revolution of 22–24 February 1848; in part 3, it is the coup d'état of 2 December 1851. In part 1, however, it is a private event, Frédéric's news of his inheritance.

This structural equivalence between the enrichment of a single individual and two changes of regime seems strange and even impertinent: what are we to make of the series "inheritance—revolution—counter-revolution"? Its incongruouity can be read as a comment on the excessive importance the inheritance has in Frédéric's life. In a larger sense, the parallel points to the importance of vast private fortunes—especially those that are unearned—to the pre-1848 bourgeoisie, the class whose social and political legitimacy will be virtually destroyed by the events occurring between 1848 and 1852. At the end of parts 2 and 3, major turning points in Frédéric's life will coincide with the political upheavals, but at the end of part 1, no public event parallels his private frenzy of joy. The reader has every reason, however, to be skeptical of his sudden resolve to conquer Madame Arnoux and pursue a diplomatic career, for he will be returning to the same sort of Parisian life already recounted in chapter 5, the only difference being that he will be able to afford more material comforts. The inheritance brings part 1 to a dramatic close, but by enabling Frédéric to go to Paris and do nothing, it also leads to the boredom and repetition that make part 2 such a challenge to readers, and that make *Sentimental Education* such an exasperatingly rewarding novel.

9

Struggle

Flaubert's abandoned title for part 2, *La Lutte,* is probably the least appropriate of the headings from his early scenario, at least if we take it to refer to Frédéric Moreau. Rather than struggling to succeed, or fighting to win the objects of his desire, the novel's central character reacts—often passively—to events, and lets his life be structured by the actions of others. Nowhere is the lack of direction in Frédéric's life more apparent, or more frustrating to the reader, than in part 2. The boredom and disconnectedness that many readers complain of in *Sentimental Education* are primarily a problem in the novel's long middle, where it sometimes seems that the true struggle is that of the reader, trying to get through it all. While writing the novel, Flaubert was worried about the weakness of his characters and the complexity of his plot, and recognized that he might not be doing enough to maintain his readers' interest in the story. He nevertheless believed that his characters and the structure of his book were profoundly true to his subject matter, namely the slow disillusion of a group of very ordinary men in a world dominated by money, vanity, and empty ideals.

Part 2 begins with the arrival in Paris of Frédéric, newly rich, and confident that now he will be able to possess Madame Arnoux. This belief that his money and social position will help him win her suggests that his great love is already contaminated by the logic of prostitution. The degradation of Frédéric's ideal becomes complete at the end of part 2 when he substitutes Rosanette for Madame Arnoux in the love nest he has rented, charming the courtesan with the flowers, lace, and slippers purchased to impress the woman of his dreams. Between these memorable and strongly related moments, however, the narrative moves through myriad incidents whose interest is far from obvious, and whose relation to one another can be difficult to grasp, especially on first reading. All but one of the six chapters are long, and four of them (2, 3, 4, and 6) are collections of scenes that have little unity, so that the chapter breaks seem to be empty formal devices, which at most highlight a few particular events, but do not provide graspable narrative units.

This narrative form is important because it suggests to the reader that Frédéric's life lacks direction and that no one aspect of his existence and activities is any more authentic or important than another. Flaubert's belief in the fitness of style to subject matter leads him to reject the option of simply having the narrator tell about Frédéric's passivity and indecisiveness; instead, the tangential transitions, discontinuities, and uninterpreted details provide the reader with a simulation of the way in which Frédéric experiences the people around him and the events that occur in his life.

With no single strong plot line, and chapters that are themselves collections of disparate elements, part 2 of *Sentimental Education* consists essentially of a long succession of scenes, units of description and dialogue pertaining to a gathering of characters in a particular place. These scenes are usually quite unrelated to those they follow and precede. Strong resemblances between certain scenes, however, enable the reader to group them into several series. For example, Dussardier's punch party (chapter 6) recalls Frédéric's housewarming (chapter 2), and both of them belong to the series of meetings and conversations involving Frédéric's circle. Frédéric's meetings with Madame Arnoux form another series, as do his visits to Rosanette's; these two series are linked by both the contrast between the two women and the circulation of objects (via Arnoux) between their households. Another series of comparable scenes is formed by social events in semipublic, semiprivate spaces: Rosanette's masked ball, the Dambreuse receptions, and in a sense the horse races on the Champ de Mars as well. These groupings are not firm, and certain scenes could be said to belong to more than one series: the dinner at the Café Anglais and Cisy's luncheon resemble, in different ways, the meetings of Frédéric's circle, visits with Rosanette, and receptions at the Dambreuse mansion. Most of these groups of similar scenes extend into parts 1 and 3, but this form of composition is more striking in part 2 because the plot line is weaker.

The resemblances between scenes mean that they often become superimposed in the reader's mind. They also invite comparisons. Dussardier's party can be read as a reprise of Frédéric's in surroundings that are humble instead of opulent. The comparison shows that some personal relationships within the group have deteriorated with the passage of time and events, and that the resentment of the young men against the July Monarchy has grown more bitter and intense. The eclectic costumes at Rosanette's ball form a more elegant version of the jumbled architectural styles at the Alhambra, and the women at one of the Dambreuse soirées, whose variety makes Frédéric think of a harem or a bordello, are in turn similar to the masked women at the courtesan's ball. These comparisons contaminate the elegant and seemingly refined Dambreuse milieu with traces of promiscuity and prostitution. The reprise of similar scenes thus suggests insights into both the resemblances and the differences between milieus, or between an earlier and a later state of the same social group.

The metaphoric relationship between scenes suggests both the circularity and the irreversibility of time, the former because Frédéric seems to find himself repeatedly in the same kinds of situations, and the latter because these returning circumstances point to the gulf that separates past and present. Frédéric's ride down the Champs-Elysées with Rosanette after the races recalls a similar scene that he had witnessed while walking around Paris during his first year there: "Then Frédéric remembered those days, already distant, when he had longed for the ineffable joy of sitting in one of these carriages, next to one of these women. He now possessed that joy, and was none the happier" (210).

The comparison between scenes is rarely made this explicit, or attributed to Frédéric, but it is always a possibility for readers, who will often find the similarity of scenes more compelling than the plot connections between them.

The actual succession of scenes, especially in part 2, is often accomplished by transitions that are tangential and seemingly without motivation. Here, for example, is how the narrative moves from a visit with Rosanette to a conversation about Frédéric's support for a newspaper:

> He arrived home in a gloomy mood.
> Hussonnet and Deslauriers were waiting for him. (157)

Scenes often begin as interruptions or distractions:

> The situation was becoming intolerable.
> His mind was taken off it by a letter from his solicitor. (179)
> While he was on his way, the thought of Arnoux and his wife assailed him once more. (194)

The transitions between scenes do not, for the most part, coincide with the causal or logical links between plot elements. The narrative thus seems to lurch forward in a series of displacements, many of them gratuitous and many others the products of Frédéric's vacillating mind. From Frédéric's perspective, which is generally the viewpoint most accessible to the reader, events seem related by little more than accident.

The tenuous connections between successive segments of the novel should not, however, lead us to conclude that its story is incoherent, discontinuous, or implausible. It is the reader's access to the story, like Frédéric's perception of so much of what goes on in his life, that is full of gaps, discontinuities, and chance interferences. Rather than a single dominant plot line with subordinate details, several distinct but interrelated plots crisscross the middle of *Sentimental Education*. These parallel plots are individually coherent, but none of them is particularly intriguing or compelling, and their intermingling makes all of them tricky to follow. Because of the connections between them, these plots cannot be

Struggle

absolutely separated from one another or precisely defined. Nonetheless, several reasonably distinct strands can be distinguished:

- Arnoux's decline and his financial dealings, in which Frédéric becomes entangled;

- the intrigues surrounding Rosanette, involving Arnoux, Delmar, Mademoiselle Vatnaz, Cisy, and Frédéric;

- relations between Frédéric, Monsieur and Madame Dambreuse, and their circle, including Martinon;

- relations between Frédéric and his friends, principally concerning their attempts to gain something from his wealth or social position;

- the intensifying social and political strain between opponents of the July Monarchy, such as Frédéric's circle, and its supporters, such as the Dambreuse circle; and

- Frédéric's attempts to become more intimate with Madame Arnoux.

Arnoux's schemes and money troubles are, in themselves, a straightforward financial intrigue of a type that, since Balzac, had been common in novels of modern life. He makes bad investments, borrows money, neglects legal formalities, and loses the confidence of his backers and the money of his wife and friends. His worst investment, made on the advice of Regimbart, is in a porcelain-clay mine in Brittany; when the company fails, Arnoux, as a director, becomes personally liable for a portion of its debts. His building sites in Belleville (now a Paris neighborhood, then a village just east of the city) involve him in a lawsuit, and he borrows heavily on them, finally using an unregistered mortgage as security for Frédéric's loan of 15,000 francs. When Arnoux is forced to sell the land for less than the value of the mortgages, Frédéric loses his money. Trying to stay afloat in the face of these bad investments, Arnoux borrows money from Dambreuse, and has his wife sign some of the loan agreements, thereby compromising her personal fortune by using it as collateral.

This plot differs from comparable dealings in Balzac novels in two major ways, both creating difficulty for readers. One is Arnoux's easy-going attitude through it all: he puts on a long face for Frédéric when he needs money from him, but otherwise shrugs his shoulders and continues to enjoy life. His lack of passion or anxiety removes the pathos that accompanies such declines in Balzac's characters and makes readers interested in them. The other difficulty is the fragmentary presentation of information on Arnoux's dealings: pieces of the story come to Frédéric —and to the reader—from Madame Arnoux, Dussardier, Rosanette, and the newspapers, and the narrator never summarizes the matter to clarify them. Frédéric learns the extent of Arnoux's difficulties only gradually, and largely by accident. It is a vaguely worrisome situation, too incidental to Frédéric to occupy much of his, or the reader's, attention. His first concern is not to understand, but to reassure Madame Arnoux. Arnoux uses the young man's affection for her to get him to lend the 15,000 francs and to intercede on his behalf with Dambreuse, but this action brings Frédéric no closer to Madame Arnoux.

In a similar fashion, the progress of the intrigues involving Rosanette and her protectors bears little relation to Frédéric's attempts to seduce Arnoux's mistress. As is customary in *Sentimental Education,* the circumstances are revealed piecemeal and incidentally, so that once again the reader's experience simulates Frédéric's gradual understanding of what is happening. In part 1, he overhears Mademoiselle Vatnaz say to Arnoux, "Farewell, happy man!" and "You are loved" (47, 82). The reader can also guess that the note from Mademoiselle Vatnaz recalling Arnoux to Paris from Saint-Cloud probably concerns one of the dealer's mistresses, because something on a paper from Arnoux's pocket upsets his wife when he carelessly uses it to wrap a bouquet for her.

Rosanette herself is introduced only at her masked ball in part 2, although she was the girl Frédéric once saw at the theater with Arnoux and a woman who turned out to be Mademoiselle Vatnaz. Both Arnoux and old Oudry act as Rosanette's protectors; Mademoiselle Vatnaz serves her as a go-between and occasional confidante, apparently in exchange for money. The two are rivals for the affection of the actor Delmar, whom Mademoiselle Vatnaz loves persistently and whose affair with Rosanette she discovers (and reveals to Frédéric) shortly after Rosanette breaks with Oudry. Rosanette alternately encourages and rebukes Frédéric, and humiliates him by going home with Cisy from the Café Anglais. She then takes up with a Russian prince and apparently buys her way back into the good graces of Mademoiselle Vatnaz, who informs Frédéric that Rosanette is again interested in him.

Frédéric's relationship to the Dambreuses, like the financial woes of Arnoux, can be said to be a rewriting of a plot characteristic of the novels of Balzac. Deslauriers, as we have noted, made this connection explicit when he urged Frédéric to become Madame Dambreuse's lover. If Frédéric is to act the part of a Balzac hero like Rastignac, he must use Madame Dambreuse, her husband, and their circle to win wealth and social position. It is crucial to remember, however, that there is a vast difference between *acting the part* of someone and *being* someone, even when both the original and the role-player are fictional characters. Balzac never shows his hero being urged to copy a fictional protagonist, but instead presents Rastignac's desire to win fortune and social prestige as the logical consequence of the contrast he sees between the life of his provincial family and the refined luxury of the Parisian elite. Frédéric is less spontaneously impressed by the milieu represented by the Dambreuses, and his intermittent resolve to frequent them is calculated and cynical: "in a sudden burst of animal health, he resolved to lead a selfish life. He felt as if his heart was as hard as the table on which his elbows were resting. Now he could throw himself into society life without fear. He thought of the Dambreuses; he would make use of them" (117). Their world in itself has only limited appeal to him, and when he first attends one of their receptions, he enjoys being in opulent surroundings, but finds the conversation tiresome and ordinary.

Frédéric only returns to see Monsieur Dambreuse because Madame Arnoux has made a casual remark approving his plan to have the banker recommend him for a position in the Council of State. Dambreuse assures him that this can be done easily and invites him to another reception, where Frédéric finds Martinon busily joining in the conservative platitudes of the conversation and being attentive to Madame Dambreuse. Her husband proposes that Frédéric go into business with him rather than attempt to enter the Council of State, and he later advises him to invest in his coal company and become his private secretary.

The Dambreuse household is for Frédéric a scene of contrasts and incongruities, never a social ideal. When he enters a room full of seated women at one of their receptions, he is struck by the revealing clothes worn in this cautious and pretentious milieu: "the respectability of their faces compensated for the daring of their dresses" (164). Like the guests at Rosanette's ball, these women form a collection of national and regional types of feminine beauty, and Frédéric silently compares them to a harem or to the women of a bordello. When he returns to the Dambreuses following his duel with Cisy and his failure to conclude the business deal, he finds the banality and conservatism of their conversation so annoying that launches into a tirade against the institutions of the July Monarchy, momentarily scandalizing the assembly with remarks such as, "I don't care a damn about business!" (241). He does not see the banker and his wife again until after the revolution of 1848, when the changed political circumstances make Dambreuse think that Frédéric might be useful to his cause.

If Frédéric's relations to the Dambreuses are based on expectations of personal gain, the same is increasingly true, in part 2, of his relations to his younger friends, especially Deslauriers. The lawyer sees Frédéric's inheritance as a good fortune in which he will share, and Flaubert deftly uses free indirect discourse to emphasize their mutual egoism: "His friend displayed too much pleasure for the two of them, and not enough for him alone" (118). Deslauriers quickly becomes obsessed with using some of Frédéric's money to start a political journal, which will be a springboard to his conquest of political power, and for a time he joins forces with Hussonnet: the two of them plead with Frédéric for the money needed to transform Arnoux's old magazine. Although Frédéric at one point agrees to provide 15,000 francs, he is hardly sorry when his loan to Arnoux forces him to go back on his commitment, because he never saw in the journal anything but an expression of the vanity and vulgar ambition of Deslauriers. Egoism for egoism, he prefers his own, and would rather buy things for himself and Madame Arnoux than subsidize his friend's career move.

The estrangement of Frédéric from Deslauriers over money is paralleled by similar developments with other members of their circle. Pellerin wants Frédéric to buy his painting of Rosanette, which neither the courtesan nor Arnoux is willing to pay for, and with the help of the others he finally succeeds in getting Frédéric to make the purchase. Sénécal expects Frédéric to get him jobs with Arnoux or Dambreuse. Hussonnet tries to avenge Frédéric's failure to provide the money for the journal by publishing a malicious account of his duel with Cisy. The ideal of a circle of young men devoted to one another's success—another situation straight out of Balzac's fiction, as Deslauriers points out (158)—collapses because of the importance of money and the absence of shared values. None of the young men admires or believes in the causes and plans of the others.

Their mutual estrangement, like Frédéric's irritation with the Dambreuse circle, is closely related to the deepening social and ideological conflict in the last years of the July Monarchy. The ever sharper attacks of the reformers, the growing resentment of the have-nots, and the ossifying conservatism of the privileged together constitute the most important and carefully developed plot of part 2. The political statements correspond closely to the background, social standing, and personal situation of those who make them. Flaubert read many newspapers and tracts from the last years of the July Monarchy so that his characters' pronouncements would fit in with what was being said at the time, and give the impression that they are often quoting the commonplaces of the day. Rather than attempting to judge overtly, Flaubert tries to display the shallowness or bad faith of each position through the words of its own supporters.

Deslauriers is the novel's most prolific speechmaker, but his convictions shift frequently, and his radicalism is opportunistic. When Frédéric returns to Paris after his years in Nogent, he finds his old friend irritated and embittered by his lack of success. Having failed a state examination in law because of his radical views on inheritance, he longs for another time, such as that of the French Revolution, when lawyers and orators could redirect society and sway the masses. Subsequent conversations reveal that the desire for power is far more important to Deslauriers than the desire for change. He "looked forward impatiently to a great upheaval in which he confidently expected to make a niche for himself" (141). When Frédéric fails to give him the money for a newspaper, Deslauriers becomes more bitter than ever. Resentful of his friend's inherited wealth, he is again attracted to the socialist ideas of his friend Sénécal, who is always his example of suffering and his model of political purity. Frédéric, who had once noted that Deslauriers was imitating the socialist's rough dress, reproaches his extremism and resentment by telling him, "You're just like Sénécal" (118, 261).

Sénécal himself is an unsympathetic secondary character, but he is extremely important to what the novel has to say about society, politics, and revolution. Flaubert makes clear that he is not a member of the working class he claims to represent, his father having been a foreman and his political initiation having come from a secondary-school teacher. His socialism, then, is born of borrowed ideas rather than of experience. He works as a mathematics tutor at several boarding schools, then as an engineer with a machine shop and with Arnoux's porcelain factory. He loses every job because of his expressions of class resentment or radical egalitarianism: he beats an aristocratic pupil, opposes the giving of school prizes, says things his employer considers inflammatory, and denounces Arnoux for his indulgence toward a worker who is his mistress. In his resentment of wealth and privilege, he is a more extreme version of Deslauriers, but whereas the lawyer wants social upheaval so that he can acquire power, Sénécal yearns for the establishment of a socialist state powerful enough to wipe out all inequality and individualism. He lives a spartan and puritanical life, abstaining from sex and disapproving of luxury, self-indulgence, and rowdiness.

When the 1848 revolution fails to accomplish its goals and the conservative reaction sets in, Sénécal reacts positively because he sees in the authoritarian bourgeois state the foundations of the authoritarian communism of his dreams. In his essay on "Flaubert's Politics," Edmund Wilson noted that for a Marxist, Sénécal's authoritarian turn could only be understood as the result of the bourgeois in him, whereas for Flaubert it is the consequence of socialism itself (Wilson, 114–15). Separating Sénécal's political commitment from his bourgeois education is difficult, however, because this education gives his socialism its abstract and doctrinaire character, and because his class upbringing separates him from the rough pleasures of nineteenth-century workers, such as getting drunk on red wine. Furthermore, Flaubert gives us no manual laborers in the novel with whom to compare him, since Dussardier, the character closest to the working class in education and sympathy, is a shop assistant and clerk, and Rosanette left her working-class origins when she was sold into prostitution. Nonetheless, Wilson's point is well taken because Flaubert explicitly presents Sénécal's authoritarianism as being derived from the socialist theories he has read and crudely synthesized, "the weighty cartload of socialist writers, those who demand for humanity the level of the barrackroom, those who would amuse it in a brothel or tie it to the counter or the bench" (141; translation modified). In the 1990s, even more obviously than when Wilson was writing in the late 1930s, Sénécal appears to be a powerful anticipation of twentieth-century historical experience, where socialism has often been "Sénécalian," and has now been abandoned in many countries precisely because its authoritarian component grew intolerable and because very few people in the modern world wish to live by self-denying, collectivist ideals.

As unpleasant a character as Sénécal may be, however, we are only getting part of the picture if we see him as merely the vehicle for a perceptive critique of socialism's totalitarian temptation. His role in the novel cannot be reduced to his character and doctrines, because the reaction of other characters to him is more interesting than he is himself. The wealthy dislike him, one might say, for all the wrong reasons. Frédéric finds him an annoyance not because he understands the dangers of authoritarian socialism but because Sénécal criticizes his pursuit of material comforts and his self-indulgence in the feelings and trappings of art. Sénécal's rough, unfashionable clothes and haircut offend Frédéric's sense of style, and he makes a cutting remark about the tutor's poor appearance (68). When Sénécal's participation in a bomb plot is mentioned at one of the Dambreuse receptions and Frédéric defends his character, a landowner replies that "a fellow who takes part in a plot can't be a good sort." The narrator then makes clear that this reaction stems not from concern for potential victims of political terrorism but from the egoism of economic privilege: "Most of the men there had served at least four governments; and they would have sold France or the whole human race to safeguard their fortune, to spare themselves the slightest feeling of discomfort or embarrassment, or even out of mere servility and instinctive worship of strength" (240). For his participation in the June 1848 uprising, Sénécal is among the prisoners packed beneath the terrace of the Tuileries under frightful, inhuman conditions, which Flaubert describes with horrifying directness. Sénécal's crude egalitarianism entails universal servitude, but the novel's characters do not react to that danger; instead, he is scorned and punished because the beneficiaries of inequality do not like to have their position criticized or challenged.

When Sénécal finally does something truly horrible, Frédéric's reaction is disconcertingly muted. His jaw drops when he recognizes the former tutor in the policeman who kills Dussardier. The narrative breaks off, for nothing can be done about Dussardier's murder, and Frédéric, the eyewitness, has nothing to say about it and no one to say it to. In the novel's final chapter, when Frédéric chats with Deslauriers about their old friends and acquaintances, he keeps silent about Dussardier's death. Frédéric asks the lawyer about his old friend Sénécal, without mentioning the atrocity he saw Sénécal commit. Deslauriers does not ask about Dussardier, nor does Frédéric volunteer that he saw him killed. In other words, the only old friend whom the two do not mention is the one who was killed by the police during the establishment of the regime—the Second Empire—under which they still live. Frédéric, who had despised and insulted Sénécal the egalitarian, says nothing about Sénécal the agent of state violence.

If Sénécal is the novel's sinister utopian, Dussardier is its goodhearted revolutionary. Almost every commentator agrees that Dussardier is the most likeable character in the book, perhaps the *only* one with whom readers can truly sympathize. Frédéric and Hussonnet first meet him, and come to his aid, when he attacks a policeman out of spontaneous anger at seeing the policeman strike a child. His hatred of the July Monarchy and of authority in general comes not from books, as was the case with Sénécal, but from his experience as an eyewitness to the Trans-nonain massacre, one of the worst incidents of brutality to occur during the workers' insurrections of the period. On 14 April 1834, during the suppression of a riot in Paris, a wounded officer being transported was shot from a window; the troops entered the building from which the shot was fired and killed every man, woman, and child they found. The sight of their bloodstained bayonets converts Dussardier to the cause of republican government, which he believes will put an end to misery and oppression.

Dussardier's politics of the heart, in Flaubert's presentation, are as appealing as Sénécal's politics of the head are chilling. The contrast between the two is well illustrated by their reaction to Frédéric's wealth at his housewarming party. Sénécal scowls and criticizes the food, the library, and the decoration; Dussardier embraces Frédéric with joy and congratulates him. Dussardier is outraged not by inequality, but by injustice, and he identifies with the suffering of political prisoners whether or not he understands or approves of their actions. When Sénécal is arrested for his role in a bomb plot, Dussardier desperately wants to rescue him from captivity and celebrates his release by giving a punch party in his one-room attic apartment. There, in the autumn of 1847, the political passions that had been expressed at the Saturday gatherings at Frédéric's in 1842 and 1843 are raised to a new intensity: "they all shared the same loathing of authority. It was a violent loathing, with no other cause than the hatred of injustice; and they mingled legitimate grievances with the most ludicrous grumbles" (262).

The extremism of the talk at Dussardier's party points to the intensifying social resentment and opposition political activity in what would prove to be the last months of the July Monarchy. In the novel, the period immediately before the February revolution is marked above all by Frédéric's idyllic visits to Madame Arnoux in Auteuil, but in January 1848, the narrator reminds us that Frédéric had become so bitter that "like Deslauriers he longed for a general upheaval" (273). An intensification of political passions is also suggested by the increasingly reactionary talk at the series of Dambreuse receptions. When Frédéric goes there soon after his return to Paris in December 1845, there is no political conversation. On his next visit, early in 1847, he finds vague discussions of both archaic and up-to-date political topics. When Frédéric joins the Dambreuse guests again in late June 1847, their denial that society has a responsibility to the poor drives Frédéric to his outburst of radical sentiments.

Of all the plot lines developed in part 2 of *Sentimental Education*, the least coherent is the one that, at least from Frédéric's viewpoint, is the most important: the development of his relationship with Madame Arnoux. As was noted at the beginning of the present chapter, part 2 begins with Frédéric hoping to use money to win her love, and ends with him sobbing because the woman his money has finally helped him to obtain is not Madame Arnoux but the venal Rosanette. He desires Madame Arnoux intermittently and pursues her sporadically, squandering many of the fortuitous occasions when circumstances seem right for him to please her or declare his love. Their chaste intimacy during the last months before the February revolution and Frédéric's plan to become her lover in a furnished apartment do not culminate a progressively developing relationship but are contingent upon largely unrelated events.

Frédéric's first meeting with Madame Arnoux after his inheritance and return to Paris is a severe disappointment to him; his great love seems ordinary in her new surroundings. She is not even mentioned until the prospect of becoming Rosanette's lover makes him think of her. He becomes her confidant concerning Arnoux's infidelities and financial troubles, but he does not take advantage of her frustration with her husband to try to become her lover. Frédéric is so timid with her that opportunities for intimacy keep turning into periods of frustration, and try as we may to remind ourselves that his mood changes are consistent with his indecisive character, the narrative seems all but incoherent. Just after a passage in which Frédéric feels more in love with, and closer to, Madame Arnoux than ever before, chapter 3 begins with the words, "A wretched existence now began for Frédéric. He was the parasite of the house" (173). Yet within a few paragraphs, this "wretched existence" includes his success at getting Madame Arnoux to confide in him the story of her life.

Frédéric's visit with Madame Arnoux at the pottery factory near Creil is punctuated by interruptions and failures of communication. He tries to use trivial circumstances as pretexts to speak of his love, but Madame Arnoux at first fails to understand him and then rebukes him. Returning to Paris on the train, he thinks of her insultingly and vows to forget her with Rosanette. This rejection might be the end of their story but for the ironic actions of two other characters. By revealing Frédéric's plans to marry Louise Roque during his crude attempt to seduce Madame Arnoux, Deslauriers unwittingly makes her realize that she loves Frédéric. Louise's desire for two statues from the Arnoux shop sends Frédéric back there, and in the course of denying his intention to marry he declares his love to a delighted Madame Arnoux. The chaste intimacy of their visits in Auteuil follows.

At this point the love plot begins to parallel the political plot: Frédéric's sexual frustration, which he denies, seems to be expressed in his wish for a "general upheaval" of society. He gets Madame Arnoux to agree to meet him in the center of Paris, and he makes plans to entice her to a furnished apartment. The day of their rendezvous, 22 February 1848, is also a day of mass protests against the prohibition of a reformist banquet by the government of Louis-Philippe. Frédéric's passion for Madame Arnoux and his wish for sexual relations now parallel the aspiration for freedom and the lust for power of the July Monarchy's opponents. When Madame Arnoux fails to come to the rendezvous and does not answer a message the next day, Frédéric feels "a longing to indulge in violent action" and roams the streets as the revolutionary fighting begins (281). When he visits Rosanette, his timidity has vanished, and when she expresses surprise at his boldness, he wittily identifies the change in himself with the reform movement that has precipitated the momentous events of the day: "I'm following the fashion. I've reformed" (282). The shooting on the Boulevard des Capucines, the act of repressive violence that seals the fate of the July Monarchy, induces Rosanette to seek shelter with Frédéric in the apartment he had prepared for Madame Arnoux. During the night, while gunfire rocks the city, Frédéric sobs because he has possessed the wrong woman. The inescapable implication of this moment is that the republican bourgeoisie and the workers have unleashed the wrong revolution.

This parallel, which only appears at this decisive moment in the action, gives the novel a newfound coherence and sense of direction. Retrospectively, Frédéric's romantic passion for Madame Arnoux seems metaphorically related to the idealistic desires for freedom and justice that fired the reform politics of the 1840s, whose progress was no more coherent or direct than that of Frédéric's sentimental education. The overthrow of the July Monarchy, like Frédéric's rapid transformation from a timid young man into a lover, does not seem to be the outcome of a plan or even of a causally related chain of events, but once it takes place it gives the appearance of meaning and direction to what preceded it. More important for the novel's reader, the events at the end of part 2 announce the intricate parallels between private and public destinies that make Flaubert's fictional treatment of the revolution, in part 3, one of the most fascinating achievements of the nineteenth-century novel.

10

Experience

Part 3 of *Sentimental Education* begins as Frédéric Moreau, who has finally become Rosanette's lover, leaves her on the morning of 24 February to join the crowds in the streets Paris. Flushed with his amorous success, he delights in even the coarsest manifestations of the revolution, and shares the illusions and enthusiasms of the moment. With their respective desires for sexual conquest and social upheaval satisfied, Frédéric and the republican bourgeoisie must now live out the experiences that they have so long sought. Flaubert's tentative title, *L'Expérience*, fits the last part of his novel well. The years from 1848 to 1851, in the novel and in French history, are a period of action and of disillusionment, of experiences undergone and experience acquired.

Chapter 1, by far the longest of the novel, covers the four months from the February revolution to the brutally suppressed workers' uprising known as the June Days. Flaubert's presentation of the revolutionary events has much in common with two of the most trenchant contemporary accounts, Karl Marx's *The Eighteenth Brumaire of Louis Bonaparte* and Alexis de Tocqueville's *Recollections*. Marx's pamphlet was a work of polemical historical analysis, Tocqueville's a memoir, and Marx's historical materialism could hardly be more distant, ideologically, from

Tocqueville's liberalism. However, both authors, like Flaubert, saw in the events of 1848–51 much imitation of the French Revolution of 1789–99. This insight is especially central to Marx's analysis, whose title refers to the date of the coup d'état by which Napoleon I seized power in 1799, and thus implies that Louis Bonaparte's coup d'état of 1851 is merely an imitation of his uncle's. *The Eighteenth Brumaire* begins with the dictum that "all great, world-historical facts and personages occur, as it were, twice . . . the first time as tragedy, the second as farce,"[29] and Marx proposes that the entire period from the February revolution to the nephew's coup d'état be treated as a farcical reprise of the language, slogans, and characters of the French Revolution, especially those of the Convention, the assembly that ruled from 1793 to 1795.

Tocqueville, far more empirical in temperament and outlook, says virtually the same thing, not about the entire period but about the events in the Chamber of Deputies (legislature) on 24 February:

> The quality of imitation was so obvious that the terrible originality of the facts remained hidden . . . . The men of the first revolution were still alive in everyone's mind, their deeds and their words fresh in the memory. And everything I saw that day was plainly stamped with the imprint of such memories; the whole time I had the feeling that we had staged a play about the French Revolution, rather than that we were continuing it . . . . I could not take the actors very seriously; the whole thing seemed a vile tragedy played by a provincial troupe.[30]

For Tocqueville, as for Marx, the revolutionary text is tragic, its performance unwittingly farcical.

The theatrical metaphor appears in *Sentimental Education* as soon as Frédéric ventures out into the streets of revolutionary Paris. As crowds surge and infantry companies and national guardsmen exchange fire, Frédéric "was fascinated and enjoying himself immensely. The wounded falling to the ground and the dead lying stretched out did not look as if they were really wounded or dead. He felt as if he were watching a play" (286). More specifically, Flaubert's characters, like the historical figures described by Marx and Tocqueville, take the orators of the earlier revolution as their models. Even before 1848, Deslauriers

dreamed of the power men's words had in that era, and the narrator refers to him as "the future Mirabeau" (119, 148). Frédéric in effect cop-
ies his friend's imitation when, following Monsieur Dambreuse's
suggestion, he imagines himself winning election to the National Assembly: "The great figures of the Convention passed before his eyes"
(297). Sénécal, presiding over the ironically named *Club de l'Intelligence,* provides a pretext for the narrator to comment on the ubiquity
of this sort of imitation: "as it was customary for every person in the
public eye to model himself on some famous figure, one copying Saint-
Just, another Danton, and yet another Marat, he himself tried to resemble Blanqui, who in his turn imitated Robespierre" (301).

Like the accounts of Marx and Tocqueville, Flaubert's presentation
of the February revolution has recourse to figures of confusion and contrast. Recounting the political maneuvers leading up to the monarchy's
collapse on 24 February, both Flaubert and Tocqueville use a choppy
style that suggests a jumble of things happening rather than a controlled
or organized chain of events. Flaubert: "While aides-de-camp came and
went at the Tuileries, while Monsieur Molé, who was constructing a new
cabinet, failed to reappear, while Monsieur Thiers tried to form another,
and while the King dillied and dallied, giving Bugeaud complete authority
only to prevent him from using it, the insurrection grew in strength"
(285). Tocqueville: "The leaders of both parties were absent; the former
ministers were in flight; the new ones had not appeared; there were
shouts for the sitting to begin, but they were more the expression of
some vague longing for action than of any firm plan; the President refused" (Tocqueville, 44). Flaubert's summary of the speeches in the political clubs prior to the April elections emphasizes contrasts between
intelligence and stupidity, rhetoric and idea, speaker and utterance:
"Here and there a lightning-flash of wit appeared among these clouds of
stupidity . . . a point of law was formulated in an oath, and flowers of eloquence blossomed on the lips of a workman wearing a sword-belt across
his bare chest" (300). To Marx, the incongruities observable in the February revolution stemmed from the contradiction between the aspirations
of those who had carried out the revolt and the changes that were really
possible under the circumstances. This contrast was so great that "in no

period do we find a more confused mixture of high-flown phrases and actual uncertainty and clumsiness, of more enthusiastic striving for innovation and more deeply rooted domination of the old routine" (Marx, 442).

Both Tocqueville and Flaubert saw the domination of the old routine at work in the way conservative forces moved to adopt the language of social equality without making real changes or concessions. The liberal historian wrote that "great landlords delighted to recall that they had always been hostile to the middle class and well diposed to the humble . . . the middle classes discovered a certain pride in recalling that their fathers had been workers" (Tocqueville, 78). After reading Frédéric's effusive account of the February uprising in a Troyes paper, Monsieur Dambreuse realizes that he might be able to make use of such an eloquent (but wealthy) partisan of the revolution. He and Martinon call on Frédéric to try to win him over by displaying their support for the new regime. Monsieur Dambreuse "was delighted with what had happened, and had enthusiastically adopted 'our sublime motto: Liberty, Equality, Fraternity,' for he had always been a republican at heart." Martinon "talked of his ploughman father and played the peasant" (296).

In describing the rallying of conservative individuals and institutions to the new Republic, Flaubert also had at his disposal a device that neither Marx nor Tocqueville could use, that of implying a parallel between the actions of real and fictional individuals. When Frédéric returns to Rosanette's the day after the fall of the July Monarchy, "she declared herself in favor of the Republic, a position which had already been taken up by His Grace the Archbishop of Paris, and which was to be adopted with remarkable alacrity by the Magistrature, the Council of State, the Institut, [etc.]" (293). Nowhere is it said that the Archbishop and the state institutions are prostituting themselves, but the identity of their decision to that of Rosanette makes the suggestion to the reader. The novel, unlike the works of historians, can interpret historical figures and actions by comparing them to fictional characters and plot elements. When the narrator says of Monsieur Dambreuse, after his death, that he had worshipped authority "so fervently that he would have paid for the privilege of selling himself" (373), the remark can be taken to apply not only to the individual, but also to other financiers of his ilk, and perhaps even the entire social class to which he belongs.

If the conservative elements of society are likened to prostitutes, the February revolution itself is presented in sexual terms as both a degrading violation and an idealistic infatuation. The parallel established at the end of part 2 between the revolution and Frédéric's affair with Rosanette continues to inform the narration as Frédéric observes and joins the throngs in the street and the Tuileries Palace. His lighthearted enjoyment of the street fighting shows him still in the same mood as when he seduced Rosanette while talking of his "reform." When Hussonnet grouses about the odor and the vulgar behavior of the people invading the palace, Frédéric is irritated, and finally tells him, "I don't care what you think . . . I think the people are sublime" (290). To him, the people's romp through the palace is a joyous transgression comparable to the one he has just enjoyed with Rosanette. The takeover of the palace includes an act of symbolic violation: "Jailbirds thrust their arms into the princesses' bed, and rolled about on it as a consolation for not being able to rape them" (289). Frédéric and the people of Paris are realizing the transgressive desire of Oedipus, but with degraded, substitute objects. Those who have deposed the king, symbolically a father to the nation, are acting out the possession of women from the royal family by ransacking their bedrooms; Frédéric, who had treated Arnoux as a substitute father and desired Madame Arnoux as a maternal ideal, has now become the lover not of Arnoux's wife but of his mistress. The parallel between Frédéric and the people is underscored by the fact that Arnoux himself is the bravest of the national guardsmen who are defending the palace apartments from further violation at the hands of the crowd. The next day, Frédéric strolls through the city with Rosanette, proud to be seen with her, his mood mirroring the pride of the people of Paris in their newly won rights.

A brief comment is in order on the word *peuple* (people) and its translation. Like its English counterpart, *peuple* can designate all the members of a nation, as in "We, the people . . ." or "*Au nom du peuple français . . .*" ("in the name of the French people"). No less important, *le peuple* also means the masses, the common people, the lower classes, the proletariat—a usage that is much less accepted in democratic-minded

America. The word can, in addition, designate a crowd or an assembled multitude, but it is never used as the plural of *person,* or in the sense of "some individuals" or "human beings." In Robert Baldick's version of *Sentimental Education,* a variety of words (italicized in these examples) are used to translate the word *peuple:*

> Fresh groups of *workers* kept coming up . . . . (287)

> It was the *mob.* (288)

> "What a myth!" said Hussonnet. "There's the sovereign *people* for you!" (289)

> . . . the *mob,* less out of vengeance than from a desire to assert its supremacy, smashed or tore up mirrors . . . . (289)

> Taking off their policemen's caps, and revealing their somewhat bald heads, they bowed low to the *mob.* (290)

> 'I find the *common people* revolting.' (290)

> 'I think the *people* are sublime.' (290)

> 'All is well! The *people* have won!' (291)

The most striking of these uses of the word *peuple* is the second, which refers to the arrival of an angry crowd in the Tuileries Palace: *"C'était le peuple."* Here the political abstraction suddenly becomes concrete: the Monarchy is overthrown, and the Republic proclaimed, in the name of the people, but the unwashed masses ransack the palace. In the subsequent uses of the word *peuple,* Flaubert continues to play on the dissonance between the people as idealized collectivity and the people as lower-class mob.

In the final example given above, however, we find no tension between the meanings of *le peuple,* for the speaker is Dussardier, who believes unreservedly in the identity of the nation and the masses. Unlike Frédéric, who has substituted Rosanette for Madame Arnoux,

Dussardier believes that he has won his ideal love, the Republic. While in the King's absence the masses ravage his palace, and in Arnoux's absence Frédéric takes his mistress, Dussardier, more universal and idealistic in his desires, feels that in the absence of all kings humankind will enter a paradise of happiness and freedom: "The Republic has been proclaimed! We shall all be happy now! . . . No more kings! You understand what that means? The whole world free! The whole world free!" (291). Dussardier at the Tuileries evokes the lyrical illusion of revolution in its purest form: for him, this sudden, ecstatic moment of social harmony ("Workers and bourgeois are embracing!") and liberation ("The people have won!") will change the world forever. He is inarticulate with joy, for the revolutionary moment seems to transcend all ordinary concerns, such as his own wound or the fact that his friends, whom he congratulates on their part in the fighting, are unarmed. Only the prospect of participating in yet another moment of liberation, this time that of the forts of Paris, brings him out of his ecstatic vision.

Caught up in the enthusiasm of both his own amorous conquest and the people's conquest of freedom, Frédéric for a time shares Dussardier's joyous illusions. He writes—and is imprudent or opportunistic enough to sign—a "lyrical account of the recent events" for a newspaper at Troyes, near his home town of Nogent. When Monsieur Dambreuse invites him to prepare an electoral speech, he articulates a social policy based on the unlimited generosity of the wealthy, who are asked to accept heavy taxation to support universal education and, above all, enormous subsidies for the arts. Dambreuse, of course, is the enemy of this kind of revolution, and he decides to become a candidate himself. Frédéric loses his illusions about his own possible role in the revolution at the *Club de l'Intelligence,* where he is denounced for his failure to join his friends in the demonstrations on 22 February. The Club's meeting is a cacaphony of slogans, utopian dreams, special pleading, and earnest expressions of solidarity and ideological purity. The resentful fervor and absolute lack of realism of the debates are perhaps best exemplified when a gaunt worker proclaims in a "tragic voice" that "the Government ought to have issued a decree by now, abolishing prostitution and poverty" (305). Frédéric, who despises the collective level of talk at the Club and cares only about his own speech, is finally thrown out as an "aristo" when he objects to an expression of solidarity delivered in Spanish.

The most complex treatment of the failures of both Frédéric and the 1848 revolution comes in the account of the June Days, during which Frédéric and Rosanette are sightseeing at Fontainebleau. This seemingly idyllic interlude begins when Frédéric has "an urge to leave Paris" (318). He has both political and private reasons for wishing to do so. On the streets of the city, grim and bitter workers are gathering to protest the now-conservative government's decision to close the National Workshops, which had been providing many of them with subsistence, and to give them, instead, a choice between the Army and agricultural labor far from Paris. Their horror at the idea of leaving the capital recalls Frédéric's earlier insistence that it was the only place he could live, but now, while the workers wish to remain at the country's political center, Frédéric wishes to get away from it. Having failed to find a suitable political role either on the right (Dambreuse and Martinon) or the left (Sénécal's club), Frédéric turns away from the ominously approaching conflict.

Frédéric's private reason for leaving Paris is his rivalry with Arnoux over Rosanette. The tension between them is played out in comic scenes, such as their meeting on the staircase outside her apartment and Arnoux's scheme to have Frédéric take his place with the National Guard so that he can have Rosanette to himself. This incident introduces an Oedipal fantasy: Arnoux returns to the guardhouse and falls asleep with his rifle pointed at his chest, while beside him Frédéric dreams of firing the gun and then eloping with the widowed Madame Arnoux. His excursion to Fontainebleau with Rosanette appears to be a symbolic substitute for the travel and intimacy with Madame Arnoux about which he had just fantasized.

The trip to Fontainebleau may seem at first to propose a charming alternative to the sordid and harried existence of Paris. In contrast to the frenzied and snobbish pursuit of elegance that dominates life in the capital, here are the simple, rustic pleasures of the countryside. While Paris is torn by class warfare, which pits the follies of Sénécal's club against the stupid greed of Dambreuse's drawing room, Frédéric and Rosanette contemplate the treasures of French history and the beauties of nature. Their enjoyment, however, is presented as a form of escapism, always menaced by the return of what they are trying to repress—modernity, politics, the artificiality of urban life.

Frédéric and Rosanette begin their excursion with a visit to the palace, a royal residence dating from the Renaissance. Its richly decorated rooms are named for the kings of France and the rituals of court society. This symbolic museum of the Old Regime, however, confuses Frédéric and means nothing to Rosanette. The weighty sublimity of the palace only makes her yawn. Her ignorance reveals her lack of education, but Frédéric's historical knowledge, typical for a person of his social standing, does not enable him to understand his perceptions of the palace or even organize them. The history inscribed in the monumental building weighs down on him without inspiring him to make sense of it or participate in it. The many reminders of Diane de Poitiers, mistress of King Henry II, awake in him "an indescribable feeling of retrospective lust" (320), which suggests that his interest in the past is little more than a futile desire to possess what cannot be obtained. Diane de Poitiers seems no different than the courtesans and luxury goods that excite Frédéric's desire in Paris. His "retrospective lust" can also be read as merely a more sophisticated version of the desire that led the rabble to its symbolic violation of the royal princesses during the sack of the Tuileries in February.

Although Flaubert does not use the word *tourists* to describe them, Frédéric and Rosanette clearly experience both the palace and the forest in ways that are characteristic of modern tourism. Their delight in the rusticity of their surroundings could only be felt by city folk intent on romanticizing the countryside. For example, the "harsh wine, hard bread, and jagged knives" of their meal at a country inn "increased their pleasure, added to the illusion" (324). In their excursions, they passively and obediently look at whatever sights the servant and coachman point out to them. These sights are grouped in jumbled collections without unity or meaning: "The apartments of the queens, the Pope's oratory, the François I gallery, the little mahogany table on which the Emperor signed his abdication" (319); "The Siamese Twins, the Pharamond, the King's Bouquet" (321). The historical figures associated with the palace form no less heterogeneous a collection for Frédéric, despite the fact that they are listed in chronological order: "He felt the dead crowding round him and jostling him . . ." (320). Both history and nature are reduced to sets of discrete, disjointed images with which the tourist can do nothing except encumber his or her memory. In this respect, Frédéric's experience of Fontainebleau repeats his earlier experience of Paris, the place he has left. As for Rosanette, her inability to escape a life defined by the city is evident in her misery at having to stumble over tree roots and her corresponding pleasure at finding a tavern in the middle of the countryside.

Rosanette's tavern is but one of many reminders of civilization and modernity that interrupt the attempted flight into archaic and supposedly natural surroundings. While looking at scenery, the lovers see a telegraph tower and hear the sounds of quarrymen at work. When they feel themselves to be utterly alone, a gamekeeper comes by; during the idyllic moments when they lie in the grass gazing adoringly into each other's eyes, they hear the drumroll of the call to arms for the defense of the capital against the workers' uprising. Their reaction to such reminders of the troubles in Paris underscores the escapism of the trip to Fontainebleau. When travellers inform them of the battle bloodying Paris, "Rosanette and her lover were not surprised" (322). "Frédéric Moreau" might have cared about the events in Paris, but "Rosanette's lover" surely does not, and that is all that he is in Fontainebleau. His reaction to the drumrolls is even more egotistical: "'Why, of course! It's the insurrection!' Frédéric would say with a disdainful pity, for all that excitement struck him as trivial in comparison with their love and eternal Nature" (325). The forest and rocks are indeed grand and permanent, but the lovers' interest in them is narcissistic, an evasion of social reality and human history. The June Days make the romanticization of nature seem a sham.

Frédéric's decision to go to Fontainebleau on the eve of the workers' uprising further advances the parallel already established between his life and the actions of the liberal bourgeoisie in 1848. Having wished for reformist change, the middle-class supporters of the February revolution are unable to moderate the conservative, rural-dominated National Assembly, and unwilling to ally themselves with the radical economic demands of the workers. The June Days shatter all remaining hopes that a republic dominated by middle-class interests could somehow be socially progressive. The more worldly and cynical members of the class, like Hussonnet in the novel, will embrace the reaction and ally themselves with those, like Martinon and Dambreuse, who had never wanted a revolution in the first place. Those who are more sensitive and less active can only try to turn away and avoid thinking about what the February revolution has become. Frédéric thus drops out of history for a time and tries to surround himself with nature, love, and historical monuments.

His egotistical disdain for the slaughter taking place in Paris cannot simply be read, however, as an indication that Frédéric and his class have become disillusioned and selfish since February, for the Fontainebleau episode is a more elaborate reenactment of the dinner and stroll in the streets that Frédéric and Rosanette enjoyed during the beginning of the revolution. Upon hearing the shooting on the Boulevard des Capucines, Frédéric had said "calmly": "Ah! They're killing off a few bourgeois," and the narrator comments that "there are situations in which the kindest of men . . . would watch the whole human race perish without batting an eyelid" (283). The bad faith of the June Days, at least as far as Frédéric is concerned, was already present at the outset of the February revolution. Moreover, the "pride in a freer life" felt by Frédéric and Rosanette while contemplating the forest is a repetition of the "pride in a hard-won right" felt by the Parisian people after Louis-Philippe had been overthrown, when Frédéric had strolled through the streets with Rosanette on his arm. The attempt to flee from the making of history into the pleasures of private life is the logical culmination of a revolutionary enthusiasm founded on personal resentments and dreams.

The Fontainebleau idyll ends abruptly when Frédéric's concern for Dussardier, who has been wounded in the fighting, makes him once again care, however ineffectually, about the fate of his country. He arrives in a convulsed Paris, where he is taken into custody by the National Guard in an atmosphere of confusion and suspicion. Frédéric finds his friend in the care of Mademoiselle Vatnaz. Dussardier's devotion to the Republic had led him to join the National Guard, and he received his wound while fighting against the workers' insurrection. Now, for the first time, the simple and honest young man's conscience is troubled: shouldn't he have fought with the workers against the conservative interests who wrapped themselves in the flag of the Republic while actually hating it? Dussardier is beginning to realize that, as Marx wrote in *The Eighteenth Brumaire,* "the defeat of the June insurgents . . . had shown that in Europe there are other questions involved than that of 'republic or monarchy'" (Marx, 444). Dussardier's action makes him a hero—not to the workers with whom he sympathizes, but to the reactionaries who dine with the Dambreuses. The honest employee's involvement with the self-interested and deceitful Mademoiselle Vatnaz underscores the degradation of his faithful love for the idea of a republic and parallels Frédéric's substitution of Rosanette for Madame Arnoux.

Flaubert's treatment of the June Days concludes with a horrifying account, largely based on memoirs from the era, of cruelty to the men taken prisoner for their part in the uprising. It is a ferocious denunciation of reactionary violence, and serves as a pendant to the wicked satire of revolutionary fervor in the scene at the *Club de l'Intelligence.* Monsieur Roque's murder of a starving youth crying for bread is derived from two incidents described in Flaubert's reading notes on the June Days: "At the Ecole Militaire an officer was shooting through a cellar vent at the wretches who were demanding bread, and asked with a sneer, after killing one of them: 'Who is still hungry? I'll give him something.'" In the Tuileries cellar, "an innocent provincial landowner killed by a national guardsman through the grating. His brain stayed stuck to the trough and his body lay there for more than 12 hours."[31]

In the novel, the gunshot to the brain becomes the response of old age and money to the cries of youth and hunger. Monsieur Roque's victim is an impoverished version of Frédéric at the beginning of the novel: a youth with long hair. The reader must assume an active role in realizing the horror of the act by figuring out what is the "something white" that remains on the edge of the grating after the shot is fired and the young man disappears. Many readers of 1869, not surprisingly, would have preferred not to be reminded that such things had been done in the defense of the social order in which they lived and prospered. In a letter to George Sand after the novel's publication, Flaubert wrote that "the

Experience

Rouen bourgeois are furious with me because of old Roque and the cellar of the Tuileries. Their opinion is that 'the publication of such books should be forbidden' (I quote verbatim), that I favor the Reds, that I am guilty of fanning revolutionary passions, etc. etc." (*Letters*, 2:136). Flaubert considered socialism to be a misguided and archaic dream, but the sarcasm with which *Sentimental Education* mocks Sénécal and Mademoiselle Vatnaz is more than matched by Flaubert's hatred of the bourgeoisie, which is given free reign in the final pages devoted to the June Days.

Chapter 2 of part 3 returns to Frédéric and his relations with the women in his life. A dinner party given by the Dambreuses brings him together with Louise Roque and Madame Arnoux under the watchful eye of the hostess, who is being abandoned by Martinon and is eyeing Frédéric as a possible new admirer. The presence of Arnoux, Pellerin, and Hussonnet indicates the political realignments taking place following the shocks of the revolution: Dambreuse, the one-time pillar of the July Monarchy, now welcomes members of the former republican opposition who are casting their lot with the Party of Order, as the antisocialist forces came to be known. Even Deslauriers, the former radical, will serve as Monsieur Dambreuse's political operative and as his wife's lawyer, with the former socialist Sénécal serving as a business agent under his control. Rosanette herself, the only woman involved with Frédéric who is not received by the Dambreuses, will come to resemble them in that her drawing room will become a meeting place for political reactionaries.

The remainder of part 3, with the exception of the two short epilogue chapters, takes place during the Second Republic's conservative years, from June 1848 to December 1851. Frédéric's life in these years is largely divided between Rosanette and Madame Dambreuse, with Madame Arnoux reduced to the status of a haunting memory and occasional preoccupation. He more or less carries out the Balzacian plan of ambition that Deslauriers had traced for him by becoming Madame Dambreuse's lover, courting her not for love or lust but because he sees in her a steppingstone to worldly success. As he grows more attentive to Madame Dambreuse, her husband becomes more attentive to him, and he becomes a trusted adviser and confidant to the banker. Frédéric's seduction of Madame Dambreuse is calculated and artificial, virtually a parody of conventional seduction scenes. To simulate passion, he thinks of Madame Arnoux or Rosanette while he is with her.

The narrator suggests that Frédéric's sense of morality is dulled by his simultaneous love affairs with Madame Dambreuse and Rosanette. His interest in the banker's wife is above all a desire to succeed in her milieu, a desire that leads Frédéric to sacrifice what little intellectual integrity he still had to the charms of prestige and comfort: "The political verbiage and good food began to dull his sense of morality. However mediocre these people might seem to him, he felt proud to know them and inwardly longed to enjoy their esteem. A mistress like Madame Dambreuse would establish his position in society" (359–60). His double life with the two women, and the lies he must tell to each of them, become a further source of morally corrupt pleasure, with Frédéric enjoying the feeling that he is getting away with something: "'What a swine I am!' he said to himself, glorying in his wickedness. . . . Soon his lies began to amuse him" (366, 382). He justifies his deceptive and exploitative behavior toward the two women as a compensation for his inability to possess his great love, who continues to haunt his thoughts. He barely sees Madame Arnoux in part 3, and their one tête-à-tête leaves him both closer to her and farther from her than ever. They confess their love and embrace, but Rosanette arrives and escorts Frédéric away, thereby confirming Madame Arnoux's worst fears about her young admirer's devotion to her husband's mistress (354).

Frédéric's life with his two mistresses makes Part III, even after the extraordinary chapter devoted to the 1848 revolution, more event-filled than the first parts of the novel. The death of Monsieur Dambreuse provides an occasion for portraying the life of his household and his class as one of sordid emptiness and hypocrisy; the birth and death of Frédéric and Rosanette's baby show the falsity and triviality of their relationship.[32] A series of financial intrigues involving most of the novel's characters also contribute to the gradually accelerating momentum of the plot. Mademoiselle Vatnaz sues Rosanette, who tries to recoup her losses by suing Arnoux with the help of Deslauriers and Sénécal. An associate of Regimbart's, Mignot, obtains a judgment against Arnoux, who must flee Paris for want of 12,000 francs. In an unsuccessful attempt to prevent Madame Arnoux's departure, Frédéric borrows the money from Madame Dambreuse, claiming that he needs to make restitution of a sum stolen by Dussardier. When Madame Dambreuse learns (from her seamstress, Madame Regimbart) of Frédéric's real intention, she hires Deslauriers to pursue Arnoux and his wife for some old debts to her late husband. This suit leads to the auction sale of the Arnoux household goods, for which Frédéric wrongly blames Rosanette and decides to leave her.

The sale of Madame Arnoux's belongings is the climactic scene in the story of Frédéric's life; its political counterpart is the murder of Dussardier a few days later. Frédéric notices the date of the sale, 1 December, which permits the reader to place it on the eve of Bonaparte's coup d'état against Second Republic. Madame Dambreuse brings Frédéric to the sale to mock and insult his continued affection for Madame Arnoux, and she succeeds beyond her expectations. The sale provides the most intense instance of the malaise or nausea experienced by Frédéric throughout the novel when confronted with the noise, the atmosphere, the crowding, and above all the undifferentiated mixing of people, objects, and sensations characteristic of Paris. Moreover, the sale and Madame Dambreuse's purchase of a little silver casket are the culmination of a promiscuous circulation of objects (including this casket) among Rosanette, Arnoux, and his wife that has left Frédéric confused and/or disgusted throughout the novel. Because his feelings for Madame Arnoux have always been expressed in his feelings for the objects around her, the dispersal of these objects is for him like a dismemberment of her person and a profanation of his great love.[33] The complicity of that love in a general logic of venality and prostitution is underscored by the fact that Madame Arnoux's things are not only scattered, but sold to the highest bidder. Madame Dambreuse's purchase of the silver casket is not so different from Frédéric's many purchases at the Arnoux boutique, his attempt to possess something of Madame Arnoux via the objects around her.

In breaking with Rosanette and then Madame Dambreuse, Frédéric chooses fidelity to an imaginary ideal over concrete satisfactions. This choice, however, leaves him more egotistical and less idealistic than ever when news of the coup d'état arrives the next day: "Politics left him indifferent, he was so preoccupied with his own affairs" (409). Like the vast majority of his class and of the supporters of the February revolution, Frédéric barely reacts to the coup d'état: he spends two days indoors, and when he ventures out on the evening of Wednesday, 3 December, his indignation is reserved not for authoritarian rule but for the stupidity and hatred expressed by individuals in the streets. At this point he is disgusted with history, politics, and above all Paris, and his only desire is to return to the timeless haven of his provincial home and the naïve affection of Louise Roque. His own Parisian intrigues, however, have led to the loss of that possibility, because Deslauriers, who had been introduced to Monsieur Roque through Frédéric and Monsieur Dambreuse, has just married Louise. Frédéric, "shamefaced, beaten, crushed," returns to Paris in time to see Sénécal murder Dussardier.

Dussardier dies not for the Second Republic, which had long since failed to satisfy him, but for the republic of his generous but naïve dreams. Just as Frédéric sacrifices wealth and social position to his one-time ideal, Dussardier risks and loses his life out of devotion to a cause that he knows is lost. In June 1851, he had confessed his despair to Frédéric: "Isn't everything over now? When the revolution came, I thought we'd all be happy. You remember how wonderful it was—how freely we breathed! But now we're worse off than ever. . . . Now they're killing our Republic. . . . What villainy! . . . Yet if only people tried! With a little good faith, they could reach an understanding. But it's no use. . . . Personally, I've never done anybody any harm; and yet it's like a weight on my stomach. I shall go mad if it goes on! I feel like committing suicide" (392–93). Dussardier believed that a utopian future could be created democratically because he assumed that other people were essentially like him in character. Far from being typical, however, he is the most honest and selfless person in the novel, and he comes to see greed and maliciousness on both sides of the class conflict. When he cries "*Vive la République!*" during the protests against Bonaparte's coup d'état, he has apparently decided that fidelity to his ideal, however useless or even suicidal it may be, is the only decent action open to him.

Pierced by Sénécal's sword, Dussardier falls with his arms outstretched, forming a cross (411). (The French text uses the expression *les bras en croix,* whereas Baldick's translation has simply "his arms spread out.") This figure of the republican as martyr is but one of several indications that Flaubert uses Dussardier to rewrite episodes of Hugo's *Les Misérables* (1862) and comment on Hugo's treatment of republican and revolutionary politics. Hugo was the most famous and intransigent opponent of the Second Empire, having shown no inclination to compromise and return from the exile to which he had fled in December 1851. As a symbolic gesture, Dussardier's suicidal *"Vive la République!"* parallels Hugo's intractable exile and his poetic invectives against Bonaparte. It is disconcerting, then, to note that the name *Dussardier* resembles that of the vile, self-interested rogue of *Les Misérables, Thénardier.* There is something sardonic or mocking in giving this very Hugolian hero a name that evokes one of Hugo's most memorable villains.

Dussardier's posture in death recalls a precise moment in *Les Misérables:* the death, on a revolutionary barricade, of an inoccuous old man named Monsieur Mabeuf. Mabeuf carries the red flag of the workers and students to the top of the barricade, cries *"Vive la République!"*, and is felled by a volley from the soldiers facing him. He falls with his arms forming a cross (*les bras en croix*). Flaubert's description of Dussardier's posture in his fall is an exact quotation of Hugo's description of Mabeuf. The troubling parallel between Dussardier's actions and *Les Misérables,* however, is the shop assistant's earlier role in the June Days. A national guardsman, he was wounded while striking down a boy on a barricade who was brandishing the tricolor flag of the Republic. The boy (in French *gamin,* street urchin) on the barricade brings to mind one of the most memorable and spirited characters of *Les Misérables,* little Gavroche, who dies defending a barricade while mocking the soldiers who are shooting at him. In other words, Dussardier did more than fight on the side of the conservative Republic against the workers; he performed an action that would seem heinous to anyone who had adopted the romantic view of revolutionary republicanism expressed in *Les Misérables.* For the martyr of December 1851—a figure worthy of Monsieur Mabeuf and of Victor Hugo himself—to have felled a Gavroche in

June 1848, the moral and political certitudes of *Les Misérables* must be in ruins. Dussardier dies like an Hugolian hero and dies for Hugo's cause, but he cannot *be* a romantic hero of the barricades.

The impossibility of romantic heroism in *Sentimental Education* is underscored by the reaction (or lack of reaction) to Dussardier's death, particularly when compared to that of Mabeuf in *Les Misérables*. In Hugo's novel, the insurgents venerate the old man's body; their leader makes an eloquent speech about him and takes up his blood-soaked jacket as their new flag. Mabeuf's death serves no practical purpose, but it inspires those around him to imitate his courage and defiance. The killing of Dussardier, by contrast, provokes only muted horror. The crowd feel revulsion toward the policeman, Sénécal, who kills him, but that is all. Sénécal eyes them all to warn that any challenge to him will be met with force, Frédéric recognizes him, and the chapter ends. The story of Frédéric and his friends, like the story of the political passions of their generation, has reached a dead end.

The period of amorous experience that began for Frédéric with his seduction of Rosanette is brought to a close by the near-simultaneous breakup of all his relationships with women; the experience of political change begun by the February revolution comes to an end with Bonaparte's coup d'état. The two brief chapters that bring the novel to a close ostensibly belong to part 3, but temporally they form an epilogue to the more or less continuous narrative that has followed Frédéric from September 1840 to December 1851. They provide endings not to part 3 but to the entire novel.

11

Endings

Marcel Proust wrote that "the most beautiful thing in *L'Education sen-timentale* is not a phrase, but a blank": the gap between Frédéric's recognition of Sénécal and the solemn two-word sentence, "He travelled" (*Il voyagea*), which opens chapter 6 of part 3 (Proust, 595). Proust admired the sudden change of speed with which the narration shifts from the details of Frédéric's actions to a summary of his life over 15 years. The "blank" between chapters 5 and 6, according to Proust, masterfully evokes the passage of time, and does so in a way that is not anecdotal but musical. Certainly the four paragraphs beginning with "He travelled" offer some of the most rhythmic cadences and dramatic pauses in all of Flaubert's work. The chapter's opening has an incantatory quality that invites the reader to place Frédéric's life at a distance and to consider what follows as an epilogue or conclusion.

Madame Arnoux's visit to Frédéric (412–16) is a conclusion from her point of view as well, a farewell that is, she tells him, her "last act as a woman." Perhaps nowhere else in the novel does Flaubert so successfully fuse ironic detachment and tender emotion. Free indirect discourse is used to distance the characters' words from them at crucial moments, clichés are rampant, deception is evident, and yet through it all the reader can sense the delicate mixture of immense sadness and radiant happiness that Frédéric and Madame Arnoux feel in seeing each other again, for the last time.

They tell each other their own story, delighting in shared or redis-covered memories and in confidences about hitherto unexpressed feel-ings. Yet their conversation is far from serene because they are still living the story they are telling. Much of the complexity and poignancy of the scene derives from the fact that as long as they continue to talk to each other, Frédéric and Madame Arnoux are still creating the story that they are trying to conclude. There is an ever-present possibility of a collapse of levels, by which a narrative statement about the past could become part of a seduction in the present. The sentence, "She rapturously ac-cepted this adoration of the woman she had ceased to be," captures the confusing and paradoxical temporality of the situation, in which it is nec-essary, but impossible, to maintain a distinction between the old Mad-ame Arnoux and the Madame Arnoux of old.

Frédéric's adoration is stated in conventional language and out-moded literary clichés, and would never have been expressed at all had he not needed to conceal his shock at seeing Madame Arnoux's white hair. The inauthenticity of his remarks is explicitly denounced: "Frédéric, drunk with his own eloquence, began to believe what he was saying" (414). Yet we have no reason to suppose that Frédéric's feelings are any less real than anything else in the novel simply because they are induced by verbal commonplaces. Readers of the penultimate chapter of *Senti-mental Education* should remember the narrator's rebuke to Rodolphe's dismissal of Emma's trite expressions of love in *Madame Bovary:* ". . . as if the soul's fullness did not sometimes overflow in the emptiest meta-phors, since no one, ever, can give the exact measure of his needs or ideas or sorrows, and since human speech is like a cracked pot on which we beat out tunes fit for bears to dance to, while wishing that we could touch the hearts of the stars above" (*OC*, 1:639). As Madame Arnoux de-lights in Frédéric's endearments, a worldly reader may be inclined to think that Frédéric appears better and more loving than he is, but it can also be said that through his gentle words to her, he becomes better and more loving than he was. As was noted in chapter 7, *Sentimental Educa-*

tion is not a novel in which the words of the characters' speech and thought can be confronted with an essence behind the words; instead, the characters *are* the words they speak and think. That is not to say that this novel, any more than any other, is composed of mere words instead of something more substantial. It is rather to say that characters live in and by their words, so that the kind of language they adopt matters very much. Nothing Frédéric says to Madame Arnoux in this chapter can be praised for either artistry or sincerity, and yet he achieves a state of affection and delicacy that suffices to give Madame Arnoux—to paraphrase the novel's final lines—the best time she ever had. "No woman has ever been loved as I have been loved," she says to him. As for Frédéric, "His former sufferings were redeemed"—if only for a moment, in the magical act of telling her that it is so.

The love story of *Sentimental Education* concludes with Madame Arnoux's departure, but the moral history of a generation requires an ending of its own. The conversation between Frédéric and Deslauriers in the final chapter is even more detached from the body of the novel than Frédéric's last meeting with Madame Arnoux, for their talk about the past is unrelated to their life in the present, which no longer seems to matter either to themselves or to the reader. They review the current activities of their friends and acquaintances in a tone ranging from indifference to mild curiosity. Martinon, Hussonnet, and Cisy have turned their backs on the bohemian temptations of youth for conservative, even reactionary roles among the powerful and the privileged. Less interesting and impassioned than Frédéric and Deslauriers, they have had no trouble fitting into the established order, which they had once played at contesting through eccentric lifestyles. Other characters have had a grab bag of fairly unsurprising destinies: Pellerin has tried his hand at everything, Regimbart still haunts cafés, and Rosanette is the fat widow of old Oudry.

The conversation becomes only slightly more interesting when Frédéric and Deslauriers turn to the failure of their own dreams. They try out various explanations—no straight course, too straight a course, "chance, circumstances, the times into which they were born" (418). They are obviously grasping at verbal straws, using clichés as excuses for having ended up as mediocrities. Yet it is by no means obvious that they could or should have succeeded had they lived their lives differently. Many people dream of being famous writers or powerful politicians, but the world has few places for either. Most of those who dream of glory never achieve it, not because they do something wrong but because, by definition, glory is reserved for a few. The mediocre destinies of Frédéric and Deslauriers, neither triumphant nor tragic, are surprising in a novel but common in life. Chance and circumstances are convenient excuses, but they are also part of the complex world in which many plans go astray and most dreams of distinction go unfulfilled. Far more important than these individual disappointments is the failure of the February revolution, but Frédéric and Deslauriers no longer have anything to say about politics and history. Their silence, which translates the political impotence of a society under authoritarian rule, is emphasized by their omission of the fallen Dussardier from their reminiscences.

The two friends finally console themselves by retreating into a time before the shocks of the world had dulled and disillusioned them: they exchange memories of their school days. These fond recollections concerning their masters and fellows pupils are noteworthy because, at the beginning of the novel, Frédéric and Deslauriers were described as dreamers who were almost indifferent to the school activities going on around them. As boys they lived in the future of imagination, and as prematurely old men they live in the past of memory. In other words, after 30 years, they still do not live in the present, but project themselves into another time.

The best time of all turns out to have been an interrupted visit to a brothel (418–19), an escapade mysteriously alluded to in their first conversation of the novel (part 1, chapter 2). When *Sentimental Education* was first published, critics hostile to Flaubert denounced the prominence given to this episode as a scandal. Barbey d'Aurévilly pointed to the novel's conclusion as proof of its moral "infection" (Barbey, 104). Flaubert was particularly indignant at these accusations, which he considered to be based on misrepresentation, since the two schoolboys leave the house of the Turkish woman, as she was known, no less innocent than when they entered. As George Sand stated in her review, Frédéric "thinks that the best thing in his life was escaping from his first impure action" (*Conard,* 4:701). Apparently, the critical spokesmen of bourgeois respectability were so offended by the very mention of prostitution in the context of "the best time we ever had" that they were unable or unwilling to notice the episode's real character. The ending thus functions as a trap for those who are too concerned with respectability to notice naïveté and innocence: they are condemned to misread it.

Nonetheless, George Sand's high-minded reading of the episode is itself an oversimplification. If Frédéric's flight from the bordello signifies the preservation of innocence, other aspects of the scene suggest the weaknesses that affect every aspect of his life. The act of bringing bouquets from Madame Moreau's garden implies dangerously foolish naïveté about the kind of experience to be had in a house of prostitution, and also suggests Frédéric's unacknowledged maternal fixation, which is quite obviously sublimated in his great passion for Madame Arnoux. In carrying his mother's flowers to the bordello, Frédéric acts out the same kind of degradation of his maternal ideal that can be seen in his attempts to win Madame Arnoux through money, and in his substitution of Rosanette for her in his affection. Moreover, Frédéric's indecision and timidity in front of the bemused prostitutes typifies his conduct when faced with the possibilities of life in general, and amorous relations with women in particular.

The most memorable and revealing aspect of Frédéric's and Deslauriers's visit to Zoraïde Turc's is probably the fact that "They were seen coming out. This caused a local scandal which was still remembered three years later." It is the scandal, the slander, that amuses the two young men when they recall the incident in 1840. Madame Moreau believed that Deslauriers, during summer vacation in 1837, "had taken her son to places of ill repute" (26–27), and presumably others in Nogent knew that the Moreau boy and his friend had been to "a certain street." In other words, Frédéric and Deslauriers fondly recall an occasion on which they appeared to the world as rascals without actually engaging in misbehavior. This contrast between appearance and reality provides final confirmation of Frédéric's profound ambivalence vis-à-vis bourgeois life and the conventions of respectable behavior. Through their interrupted visit to "la Turque," the two young men win a reputation as sexually experienced young libertines, when in reality Frédéric was acting like a nice young man bringing flowers from his mother's garden to his fiancée. The adventure is satisfying, and leaves only happy memories, because it satisfied a social desire—the desire to appear mature, experienced, and rakish—without involving the two young men in any of the degradations and disappointments that accompany experience throughout *Sentimental Education*.

Earlier in the novel Frédéric and Deslauriers had disagreed on the subject of their relations with women. The clerk thought that his friend should either seduce Madame Arnoux or forget about her, and affected a cynical worldliness toward women by picking up a girl in the street and by having a simple mistress, whom he mistreated. Sex and power were what mattered to him, whereas Frédéric preferred the pleasures of desire and imagination. In agreeing with Frédéric that their inconclusive escapade in the bordello was "the happiest time we ever had," however, Deslauriers seems to come around to his friend's position, namely that anticipation and innocence, given a suitably rakish disguise to impress other young men, is preferable to the prostitution, boredom, and disgust that seem to accompany experience. Half a lifetime of empty experiences have brought the two friends to agree that they were at their happiest when they stood nervously on the threshold of adult life, anticipating the pleasures of their sentimental education. The novel's ending underscores that theirs is an education without progress or profit, an inconclusive apprenticeship in the complexities of life that leads only to nostalgia and disenchantment.

Notes and References

1. Flaubert, *Correspondance*, ed. Jean Bruneau (Paris: Bibliothèque de la Pléiade, 1973, 1980, 1991), 2:437; hereafter cited in the text as *Pléiade*.

2. Flaubert, *Oeuvres complètes* (Paris: Conard, 1910–54), 14:32; hereafter cited in the text as *Conard*.

3. See David H. Pinkney, *Decisive Years in France, 1840–1847* (Princeton, N.J.: Princeton University Press, 1986).

4. Henry James, *Literary Criticism: French Writers, Other European Writers, The Prefaces to the New York Edition*. (New York: The Library of America, 1984), 331–32; hereafter cited in the text.

5. *The Letters of Gustave Flaubert*, trans. Francis Steegmuller (Cambridge: Harvard/Belknap, 1980–82), 1:154; hereafter cited in the text as *Letters*.

6. *The First Sentimental Education*, trans. Douglas Garman (Berkeley: University of California Press, 1972), 245–46.

7. Milan Kundera, *The Art of the Novel* (New York: Harper and Row, 1988), 18.

8. Barbey d'Aurévilly, *Le Constitutionnel* (19 November 1869); in *Les Oeuvres et les hommes* (Paris, 1902; rpt. Geneva: Slatkine, 1968), 18:97–98.

9. George Sand, *La Liberté* (22 December 1869). Selections from this review and several others are reproduced as an appendix to *L'Education sentimentale* in volume 4 of the Conard edition and will be cited accordingly here.

10. Marcel Proust, *Remembrance of Things Past*, trans. C. K. Scott-Moncrieff and Terence Kilmartin (New York: Random House, 1981) 1:572.

11. Marcel Proust, "A propos du 'style' de Flaubert," in *Contre Sainte-Beuve* (Paris: Bibliothèque de la Pléiade, 1971), 590; hereafter cited in the text.

12. Franz Kafka, *Letters to Felice*, trans. James Stern and Elisabeth Duckworth (New York: Schocken, 1973), 42; subsequent references in the text.

13. Gyorgy Lukács, *The Theory of the Novel*, trans. Anna Bostock (Cambridge: MIT Press, 1971), 14, 124–31.

14. Edmund Wilson, "Flaubert's Politics," in *The Triple Thinkers: Ten*

137

Essays on Literature (New York: Harcourt, Brace & Co., 1938), 113–14; hereafter cited in the text.

15. Maurice Agulhon, "Peut-on lire en historien *L'Education sentimentale?*" in *Histoire et langage dans «L'Education sentimentale»* (Paris: C.D.U. and SEDES, 1981), 35–41.

16. I am indebted to one of my students, Catherine Bordeau, for this observation. The relation of the signifiers *Moreau* and *Montereau* can be described in rhetorical terms as a *synecdoche,* a figure in which the part is substituted for the whole.

17. Maxime Du Camp, *Les Forces perdues* (Paris: Michel Lévy, 1867), 3.

18. See Naomi Schor's essay, "Idealism," in *A New History of French Literature,* ed. Denis Hollier (Cambridge: Harvard University Press, 1989), 769–74.

19. Norbert Elias, *The Court Society,* trans. Edmund Jephcott (New York: Pantheon, 1983), especially 214–67.

20. Jules Janin, "Etre artiste!", *L'Artiste* 1 (7 February 1831), 10.

21. Honoré de Balzac, *Oeuvres complètes* (Paris: Conard, 1914–40), 38: 359–60.

22. *Oeuvres complètes* (Paris: Editions du Seuil, 1964), 1:230; hereafter cited in the text as *OC.*

23. See Jerrold Seigel, *Bohemian Paris: Culture, Politics, and the Boundaries of Bourgeois Life, 1830–1930* (New York: Viking, 1986), esp. 3–96; hereafter cited in text.

24. On 5 July 1868, for example, Flaubert wrote to George Sand: "All the Christianity I find in Socialism appalls me!" *Letters,* 2:116.

25. Théophile Gautier, *Mademoiselle de Maupin* (New York: Modern Library, 1945), xxiv.

26. Pierre Bourdieu, "The Invention of the Artist's Life," *Yale French Studies* 73 (1987), 78.

27. Bibliothèque nationale manuscript N.A.F. 17611, folio 105.

28. James McPherson, *Battle Cry of Freedom: The Civil War Era* (New York: Oxford University Press, 1988), 854–58. For a discussion of contingency in natural evolution, see Stephen Jay Gould, *Wonderful Life: The Burgess Shale and the Nature of History* (New York: Norton, 1989).

29. Karl Marx, *The Eighteenth Brumaire of Louis Bonaparte,* in *The Marx-Engels Reader,* ed. Robert Tucker (New York: Norton, 1972), 436; hereafter cited in the text.

30. Alexis de Tocqueville, *Recollections,* trans. George Lawrence (New York: Doubleday, 1970), 53; hereafter cited in the text.

31. Flaubert, *Carnets de travail,* ed. Pierre-Marc de Biasi (Paris: Balland, 1988), 391–92. (Notebook 14, folio 14.)

32. Readers who follow the novel's chronology carefully will note that this

episode contains one of Flaubert's most flagrant mistakes: Rosanette is already noticeably pregnant in January 1849, but does not give birth until February 1851. This error underscores the boredom of the conservative Second Republic: Flaubert wished to end Part III with the coup d'état of December 1851, but his characters did not have enough to do during the previous three years, so he all but eliminates 1849 and 1850 by squeezing them into the time of a single pregnancy.

33. On the relations between betrayal, prostitution, and the displacement of objects and words, see Maureen Jameson, "Métonymie et trahison dans *L'Education sentimentale,*" *Nineteenth-Century French Studies,* 19, 4 (1991), 566–82.

Bibliography

Primary Sources

L'Education sentimentale was published in Paris by Michel Lévy in 1869; the two-volume edition is dated 1870. The second edition, corrected by Flaubert, was published by Charpentier in 1879 (dated 1880), and serves as the basic text for all modern editions and translations.

The best inexpensive French edition currently available is that of Claudine Gothot-Mersch (Paris: GF Flammarion, 1985), whose exceptionally fine annotation enables the modern reader to follow the many references to the historical context. Peter M. Wetherill's edition (Paris: Classiques Garnier, 1984), which is much higher priced, offers a more extensive critical apparatus, including variants from the first edition and manuscript, and a large selection of Flaubert's scenarios. The notebooks used by Flaubert during the preparation of *L'Education sentimentale* (and of several other major works) are transcribed in Pierre-Marc de Biasi's monumental edition of Flaubert's *Carnets de travail* (Paris: Balland, 1988), accompanied by remarkably rich annotation and commentary.

Other Works by Flaubert

A new edition of the complete works is being prepared for the Bibliothèque de la Pléiade collection (Paris: Gallimard) by Claudine Gothot-Mersch and Guy Sagnes. Until it appears, the standard edition remains the rather outdated *Oeuvres complètes de Gustave Flaubert* (Paris: Conard, 1910–54), 26 volumes, including 13 volumes of bowdlerized correspondence. A convenient and reasonably priced two-volume edition containing everything but the correspondence is

Bibliography

Oeuvres complètes, ed. Bernard Masson (Paris: Editions du Seuil, 1964). Three volumes of Jean Bruneau's critical and unexpurgated edition of the *Correspondance* have been published (Paris: Gallimard "Bibliothèque de la Pléiade," 1973, 1980, and 1991); they cover the period through 1868.

The following list of major works gives the date of first publication by Flaubert or, for works published posthumously, the date of completion (signaled by an asterisk).

> *Mémoires d'un fou,* 1838*
> *Novembre,* 1842*
> (First) *L'Education sentimentale,* 1845*
> *La Tentation de saint Antoine* (first version), 1849*
> *La Tentation de saint Antoine* (second version), 1856*
> *Madame Bovary,* 1857
> *Salammbô,* 1862
> *L'Education sentimentale,* 1869
> *La Tentation de saint Antoine* (third version), 1874
> *Trois contes,* 1877
> *Bouvard et Pécuchet,* 1880*

These works, with the exception of the early versions of *La Tentation de saint Antoine,* are available in inexpensive French paperbacks (GF Flammarion, Livre de Poche, and Folio collections).

Translations

Three modern translations of *L'Education sentimentale* are available in inexpensive paperback editions. Robert Baldick's *Sentimental Education* (Penguin Books, 1964) is cited herein because it is the most faithful to Flaubert's sentence structure and thus the most suitable for critical study. Perdita Burlingame's *The Sentimental Education* (New York: New American Library, 1972; now published under the Meridian Classic heading) is often very close to Baldick's version, sometimes improving on it and sometimes taking greater liberties with the syntax. Douglas Parmée's *A Sentimental Education* (Oxford: Oxford University Press, The World's Classics, 1989) is a somewhat freer and very fluid translation, generally successful and often eloquent. All have useful notes explaining historical and literary allusions, although none of them equal Gothot-Mersch's French edition in this respect.

Translations of the major novels and *November* are available. There is a two-volume selection of correspondence: *The Letters of Gustave Flaubert,* trans. Francis Steegmuller (Cambridge: Harvard University Press, 1980–82). There are also English translations of the Flaubert–Sand and Flaubert–Turgenev letters.

Secondary Sources in English

Books

Bart, Benjamin. *Flaubert.* Syracuse: Syracuse University Press, 1967. The most serious literary biography.

Brombert, Victor. *The Novels of Flaubert: A Study of Themes and Techniques.* Princeton, N.J.: Princeton University Press, 1966. Perceptive and elegant synthesis in a traditional mode; the chapter on *Sentimental Education* emphasizes the theme of prostitution.

Cortland, Peter. *The Sentimental Adventure.* The Hague: Mouton, 1967. Thorough, traditional interpretation of the novel as critique of sentimentality.

Culler, Jonathan. *Flaubert: The Uses of Uncertainty.* Ithaca, N.Y.: Cornell University Press, 1974; 2d ed. 1985. Provocative, influential study of Flaubert's narrative technique as a subversion of traditional assumptions of meaningfulness in literature.

Gans, Eric. *Madame Bovary: The End of Romance.* Boston: Twayne, 1989. A useful introduction, emphasizing close analysis of selected passages.

Haig, Stirling. *Flaubert and the Gift of Speech: Dialogue and Discourse in Four "Modern" Novels.* Cambridge: Cambridge University Press, 1986. Suggestive treatment of the direct and indirect imitation of speech in narration.

Lottman, Herbert. *Flaubert: A Biography.* Boston: Little, Brown, 1989. Reprint. New York: Fromm International, 1990. A well-researched and very readable biography, focusing on the man more than on the work.

Sherrington, R.J. *Three Novels by Flaubert.* Oxford: Clarendon Press, 1970. Studies of *Madame Bovary, Salammbô,* and *Sentimental Education,* the latter emphasizing the importance of Frédéric's point of view in the narration.

Williams, D.A. *"The Hidden Life at its Source": A Study of Flaubert's L'Education sentimentale.* Hull, England: Hull University Press, 1987. Psychological treatment of characters, emphasizing coherence and continuity.

Articles and Chapters in Books

Bourdieu, Pierre. "Flaubert's Point of View." *Critical Inquiry,* 14, 3 (1988), 539–62. Flaubert's position in the social field of literature and its relation to his aesthetics.

Bourdieu, Pierre. "The Invention of the Artist's Life." *Yale French Studies,* 73

(1987), pp. 75–103. Sociological study of Frédéric and his circle, and their relation to the social status of the artist.

Brooks, Peter. "Retrospective Lust, or Flaubert's Perversities." In *Reading for the Plot: Design and Intention in Narrative*. New York: Vintage, 1984, pp. 171–215. Engaging study of how *Sentimental Education* both relies on, and undermines, traditional novelistic plotting.

Falconer, Graham. "Reading *L'Education sentimentale*: Belief and Disbelief." *Nineteenth-Century French Studies*, 12, 3 (1984), 329–43. Incisive probing of the difficulties entailed by taking the novel *either* as the representation of a fictional world *or* as a critical deconstruction of realism.

LaCapra, Dominick. "Collapsing Spheres in Flaubert's *Sentimental Education*." In *History, Politics, and the Novel*. Ithaca, N.Y.: Cornell University Press, 1987, pp. 83–110. Suggestive analysis of how the novel interacts with and reworks the history and ideologies of its time.

White, Hayden. "The Problem of Style in Realistic Representation: Marx and Flaubert." In *Gustave Flaubert: Modern Critical Views*. Ed. Harold Bloom. New York: Chelsea House, 1989, pp. 91–109. Comparison of *Sentimental Education* and Marx's *The Eighteenth Brumaire*.

Wilson, Edmund. "Flaubert's Politics." In *The Triple Thinkers: Ten Essays on Literature*. New York: Harcourt, Brace, & Co., 1938, pp. 100–121. Insightful elucidation of Flaubert's social thought, with emphasis on *Sentimental Education*, to which Wilson compares Marx's *The Eighteenth Brumaire*.

Secondary Sources in French

Books

Butor, Michel. *Improvisations sur Flaubert*. Paris: Editions de la différence, 1984. Suggestive and wide-ranging essays by a leading novelist and critic.

Cogny, Pierre. ≪*L'Education sentimentale*≫ *de Flaubert, le monde en creux*. Paris: Larousse, 1975. Useful, eclectic commentary written for students in France, emphasizing both structure and social context.

Histoire et langage dans ≪*L'Education sentimentale*≫. Paris: C.D.U. and SEDES, 1981. A collection of essays by contemporary Flaubert specialists.

Robert, Marthe. *En haine du roman: Etude sur Flaubert*. Paris: Balland, 1982; rpt. Livre de Poche, 1984. Psychoanalytic study of the tension between realism and fantasy, with considerable attention to the relation between Flaubert's early writings and *Sentimental Education*.

Thibaudet, Albert. *Gustave Flaubert*. Paris: Gallimard, 1922; 2d ed. 1935, rpt. 1982. A classic study of theme and style in the major novels.

Articles and Chapters in Books

Oehler, Dolf. "L'échec de 1848." *L'Arc*, no. 79, pp. 58–68. Subtle, insightful analysis of the political implications of *Sentimental Education*, especially Part III.

Proust, Jacques. "Structure et sens de *L'Education sentimentale*." *Revue des sciences humaines*, no. 125, (January–March 1967), pp. 67–100. An important study of the parallel structure of personal and political events.

Proust, Marcel. "A propos du 'style' de Flaubert." In *Contre Sainte-Beuve*. Paris: Bibliothèque de la Pléiade, 1971, pp. 586–600. Perceptive essay on Flaubert's stylistic technique, with emphasis on *L'Education sentimentale*; first published in 1920.

Index

Index

The Author

William Paulson is associate professor of French at the University of Michigan in Ann Arbor, where he regularly teaches Flaubert and other French novelists in undergraduate courses. He received his doctorate in French from Princeton University, specializing in the literature of the eighteenth and nineteenth centuries. His publications in this field include *Enlightenment, Romanticism, and the Blind in France* (1987) and several articles on Balzac.

Paulson's special field of inquiry in recent years has been the relationship between literary studies and modern scientific thought; he has tried to show how insights derived from information theory and systems theory can aid in understanding the nature and function of literature in the modern world. A major part of this work was published in 1988 as *The Noise of Culture: Literary Texts in a World of Information*. His current scholarly interests include the question of literature's role in human society's relation to the natural environment.